Dedication

To Father John Kassatkin and Matushka Maxine
Kassatkin, servants of God who have dedicated
their lives to the proclamation of the Gospel and
service to the Church. Many Years! Многая лета!

PRAYING OUR FATHERS: THE SECRET MERCIES OF ANCESTRAL INTERCESSION

Keith Massey, Ph.D.

Lingua Sacra Publishing

Praying Our Fathers: The Secret Mercies of
Ancestral Intercession
Copyright © 2014 by Keith Massey

Published in the United States by Lingua Sacra
Publishing.
www.linguasacrapublishing.com
ISBN 978-0-9843432-9-4

PRAYING OUR FATHERS:
THE SECRET MERCIES OF
ANCESTRAL INTERCESSION

INTRODUCTION

You pray. Or maybe you wish you prayed more than you do. But when you pray, it's because you love your God and in prayer you spend time with the very source of our life and existence.

And you also pray because God Himself tells you in Scripture to approach Him as to a loving Father with all your needs. And you accept that God answers your prayers, giving you what you truly need, all according to His Divine Will.

But what if you've been missing something? Something huge. What if God Himself wills for you and for your good a source of spiritual blessing that you have never heard of?

What if an important type of prayer once thrived among the People of God and then somehow faded into near oblivion in almost every community of the Judeo-Christian Tradition? And what if this type of prayer is still a valid and valuable way to bring the blessings of God and His tender mercies into your life?

In this book, I will share with you the story of how I discovered the secrets of a nearly lost and forgotten type of prayer. I will explain to you that this form of prayer, called "Ancestral Intercession," is a source of "secret" mercies simply because it faded from common practice. I write this book in the hope that it will not be a secret to future generations, who will benefit from the blessings this practice can bring them.

Now, before I begin, you certainly have the right to know a little more about me and why my background might give me the credentials to make my research and opinions on a biblical topic worthy of your time.

About Keith Massey, PhD

I was born and raised in Madison, Wisconsin. I have my PhD in Biblical Hebrew and Semitic Studies from the University of Wisconsin-Madison. My minor was in Arabic. After 9/11, I served for four years as an Arabic linguist at the Top Secret National Security Agency. I was awarded the Global War on Terrorism Civilian Service Medal for service performed in Iraq in 2004.

My undergraduate studies at the University of Wisconsin-Madison were in Latin and Classical Greek. I have a Master's Degree in Old Testament from Luther Seminary in St. Paul, Minnesota.

After I left the NSA, I became a Latin teacher at a public high school. I am the author of Intermediate Arabic for Dummies, from Wiley Publishing. I have also published numerous academic articles on matters theological, biblical, and linguistic. (For a full and detailed list of my academic publications, as well as my fiction novels, please see my website: www.keithmassey.com)

All that said, I wouldn't expect you to believe anything I tell you on the basis of my credentials alone. You want to learn the whole truth, see the biblical and historical passages where I made my discovery, and then come to your own conclusions.

I am a Christian, writing this book from a Christian perspective. That said, the discovery I will describe here is something Christians, Jews, or potentially a member of any faith tradition could claim as a component of their spiritual lives.

The matters I will explore in this book, and the claims I will make, are controversial in some faith communities. It is very possible that your faith leaders will disagree vigorously with the assertions I will make here. But I will always provide you with full citations to the biblical and ancient sources I reference. Check up on me! Make sure that what I tell you is really true.

You have my respect, dear reader, and you deserve nothing short of the whole truth. And I urge you, therefore, to consider carefully the opinions of those who disagree with me. I will present the arguments they will likely make and I will tell you why I personally believe they are mistaken. In the end, you must judge for yourself what you believe is true.

If you are ready to begin a spiritual adventure, in which we will explore a mystical mystery, turn the page. We are about to travel more than three thousand years into the past. There I will tell you the story of how I uncovered the secret mercies of Ancestral Intercession.

CHAPTER ONE:
THE SECRET MERCIES OF
ANCESTRAL INTERCESSION

The story I will tell you began, as many mysteries do, with a chance encounter. Or maybe God was guiding me to make this discovery. At any rate, it would lead, by journeys through the yellowed and tattered pages of history, to the rediscovery of a nearly lost form of prayer!

As a practicing and curious Christian, and as a scholar of biblical languages and history, I read widely in topics spanning the totality of scriptural studies. I happened one day to be browsing in the Jewish Talmud. Now, Christians can and should view Jewish Rabbinical Literature as a source of information about the beliefs of 1st century Jews, certainly, but even potentially as a way to better comprehend early Christian thought.

And I stumbled there across a strange tale. Perhaps you know the story of how Moses sent spies into the Promised Land in the Book of Numbers, Chapter 13:1-33. God had brought the Children of Israel out of Egypt, led by Moses. And now they approached the land He had promised to give them. The LORD told Moses to send a representative from each of the twelve tribes to spy out the land in advance of their invasion.

When the spies returned, they reported that the land was full of high-walled cities and giants for men. They brought back a cluster of grapes so large that it took two of them to carry it on a pole. And ten of the spies declared that the land and its people were too mighty for Israel to conquer. Only two of the twelve spies, Joshua and Caleb, declared that Israel could triumph.

But the Talmud's telling of this story includes a Jewish legend not recorded in the Old Testament itself.

According to Tractate Sotah 34b of the Babylonian Talmud, as the spies traveled in the Negev (an arid region in southern Israel), Caleb left the group and went alone to the area of

Hebron. The Old Testament, in the original
Hebrew text from Numbers 13:22, does indeed
contain a curious change from a plural verb to
singular in the passage in question:

> And ***they*** went up into the Negev, and ***he***
> [Caleb alone?] came unto Hebron.[1]
>
> ויעלו בנגב ויבא עד־חברון

And so, according to the Talmud, why did
Caleb go there? He went there because he knew
that in Hebron he would find the Cave of
Machpelah, where the Patriarchs Abraham, Isaac,
and Jacob, as well as their wives, were buried.[2]
Caleb already knew that the other spies were
conspiring to make a bad report to Moses and the
Children of Israel about their prospects for victory.
And he needed help in order to resist them. And so
we read in the Babylonian Talmud Sotah 34b:

---

[1] Unless otherwise noted, translations from ancient
languages in this book are my own. I will tend to translate
literally in order to best represent the meaning of the original
text.

[2] With the exception of Jacob's second wife Rachel.
According to Genesis 35:19-20, "And Rachel died, and was
buried on the way to Ephrath, that is, Bethlehem. And Jacob
set a pillar upon her grave. That is the pillar of the grave of
Rachel to this day."

He went and he prostrated himself upon the graves of the Fathers. He said to them, "**My Fathers, seek mercy on my behalf that I may be saved from the plan of the spies**."

והלך ונשתטח על קברי אבות אמר להן
אבותי בקשו עלי רחמים שאנצל מעצת מרגלים

Caleb then held strong and resisted the plan of the others. His faithfulness was rewarded and only he and Joshua from their generation were able to enter the Promised Land after their forty year sojourn in the Wilderness.[3]

But I was dumbfounded to find a story like this in the Jewish Talmud. I believed that Jews did not engage in the practice known as Saint Intercession, that is to say, the living asking the deceased to pray for them.

I would have thought that a story which describes a practice generally condemned in the Jewish Tradition would have been edited out of the Talmud![4] The fact that this account was not

---

[3] Numbers 14:30.
[4] In Chapter Three I will describe passages from the Talmud and other early Jewish writers that argue against Saint

removed was a sign of the story's antiquity. However embarrassing the story was to later generations, just deleting it, erasing it, seemed somehow unacceptable.

And then I noticed what ended up being the most important point of all. Caleb had not asked Abraham, Isaac, and Jacob to pray for him because those men were "saints." Rather, he addressed them as "My Fathers."

He asked for their intercession *because* he was their descendant and they were his ancestors. And so I wondered, might this tale point toward some wider practice in early Judaism—and potentially early Christianity—in which people regularly asked their departed ancestors to pray for them?

In this book, I will be using the term **Saint Intercession** to refer to the more general practice of a living person asking a deceased person, whether they are a relative or not, to pray for them. But Ancestral Intercession is something different. I will be using the term **Ancestral Intercession** to describe the practice of asking a

---

Intercession.

departed direct ancestor to intercede precisely **because they are your ancestors**, not because they are saints.

Still intrigued by this curious passage from the Talmud, I set out into the earliest records of Judaism and Christianity, to see if this story about Caleb was an isolated account or whether it was part of a bigger story.

Ancestral Intercession:
The Search for Further Evidence

I was familiar with the concept of the living asking the deceased to pray for them. And this usually took the form of straightforwardly asking someone "to pray." For instance, in Latin, the prayer known as ***The Hail Mary*** includes the line:

> **Ora pro nobis** nunc et in hora mortis nostrae.
> **Pray for us** now and in the hour of our death.

But the story from the Talmud in which Caleb

asked his ancestors to pray for him contained a particular and curious idiom. Rather than saying, simply, "Pray for me," Caleb had asked them to:

"Seek" (verb: ***baqqshu*** [בקשו])
"Mercies" (noun: ***raḥamim*** [רחמים])
"On my behalf" (preposition: ***'alay*** [עלי])

I was interested in whether these particular words were used together elsewhere in the Old Testament or the Talmud to describe asking someone to pray for you. Now, we live in a world in which research that once took me months of labor in a library when I first got my PhD, now takes me mere minutes using online tools.

I searched for that precise phrase and was shocked to quickly find that the Talmud described early Jews as using that **exact same idiom** to ask their own departed loved ones to pray for them, just as Caleb asked his ancestral fathers Abraham, Isaac, and Jacob.

Here's what I found. We read in the Babylonian Talmud, Taanit 16a, in answer to a question posed as to why people go to visit graves:

In order that the dead should **seek mercies on our behalf**.

שיבקשו עלינו מתים רחמים

Notice the startling parallel between this passage and that found in the story of Caleb. In both passages, people ask the dead:

> Talmud Sotah 34b: "seek mercies on my behalf"
> Talmud Taanit 16a: "that they seek mercies on our behalf"

And in each case:

> "Seek" = **baqqash** (בקש)
> "Mercies" = **raḥamim** (רחמים)
> "On Behalf Of" = **'al** (על)

As a trained linguist, this intrigued me. Indeed, as a linguist who had worked in the Top Secret National Security Agency, searching for patterns to detect terrorist plots, this struck me as beyond pure coincidence. These passages provide us, through their common vocabulary, with the precise words that early Jews used to ask others, including their departed ancestors, to pray for them.

What Does It Mean to "Seek *Mercies*"?

What exactly does the word "mercies" (***raḥamim***) really mean in Hebrew? The word itself is plural, though usually rendered by the singular English word "mercy." It is derived from the common Semitic root that conveys the concept of "compassion" and "gentleness." The Hebrew word for womb (***reḥem***) is from this same root.

Our first instinct is usually that the word "mercy" is primarily associated with the forgiveness of sin. We have done something wrong, for which we deserve punishment. And so we ask for "mercy," meaning that we pray not to receive so harsh a response as we deserve.

And that meaning of "mercy" is indeed found in the Old Testament. For instance, we read in Psalm 79:8:

> Do not remember the iniquities of the
> forefathers against us; may **your mercies**

(***raḥameka***) come quickly to meet us.

But "mercy" in the Bible goes way beyond just asking for forgiveness of sin. Many verses point to the idea that, when you seek mercy, you can also be asking for some protection, blessing, or guidance.

Notice that when Caleb asked his ancestors to "seek mercy" on his behalf, he then immediately made a petition, "That I may be delivered from the plan of the spies." He was not seeking mercy for the forgiveness of sin at all.

Mercies for Blessings

The Bible describes "mercy" (***raḥamim***) as being the source of blessings:

According to **all that the LORD has granted us**, and His **great goodness** to the house of Israel, **which He has granted them**, according to His **mercies (*raḥamav*)**. (Isaiah 63:7)

Mercies for Guidance

We also read in the Old Testament that, when the king of Babylon had troubling dreams, he was about to kill all the wise men who could not interpret these dreams to him. Daniel asked his companions:

> ...**to seek mercies (*raḥamin*)**[5] of the God of heaven concerning this mystery, so that Daniel and his companions might not perish with the rest of the wise men of Babylon.
> Then to Daniel, in a vision of the night, **the mystery was revealed**. (Daniel 2:18-19)

Two very important things happen in this passage from the Book of Daniel. Notice that Daniel and his friends "seek mercy" *about a mystery*. And then the answer comes from God. So this is an example of *seeking mercy* meaning the same thing as *praying for guidance on an important matter*.

---

[5] This section of Daniel was written in Aramaic. The Aramaic (and Arabic) plural ending has an 'n' instead of an 'm'. But this is the same word.

But notice also that the prophet Daniel here does not consider just praying on his own to be enough. He asks three friends to also "seek mercy" from God. When it comes to prayer, there is apparently strength in numbers.

Matriarch Rachel Prays For Her Children

We read in the Mishnah, Bereishit Rabbah 82:10:

> And Rachel died and was buried in the direction of Ephrath, that is, Bethlehem. Why did Jacob our father bury Rachel in the direction of Ephrath? Because our father Jacob foresaw that the exiles would pass by there. Therefore he buried her there, **so that she would seek mercy on their behalf** (מבקשת עליהם רחמים; *mibaqqeshet 'alayhem raḥamim*).

Once again, the exact same idiom appears to describe the manner in which the dead are interceding for the living, seeking mercies on their behalf.

It would seem that the Book of Jeremiah is also alluding to the intercessory role of Rachel in the passage quoted by the Evangelist Matthew regarding the Slaughter of the Innocents:

> A voice in Ramah is heard—lamentation, bitter weeping. **Rachel weeping on behalf of her children**. (Jer 31:15, quoted in Matt 2:18)

Why Ancestral Intercession?

What have we learned so far? The Talmud suggests that some ancient Jews asked their deceased ancestors to "seek mercies" on their behalf. In the next chapter I will show you yet further evidence that this is true. But before we go any further, let's explore *why* asking our ancestors for prayer is something valuable. To do that, let's really get into the mind and heart of Caleb as he was prostrated over the grave of the biblical Patriarchs, asking them to "seek mercies" on his behalf.

Caleb in Crisis

As we read above, Caleb had been sent on the mission to spy out the Promised Land as the official representative of the House of Judah.[6] And he had become aware that ten of the other spies had a plan to make a bad report back to Moses and the Children of Israel about whether they could successfully invade and conquer the land which had been promised as an everlasting possession to the descendants of Abraham.[7] So just imagine the turmoil in his heart as all that now hung in the balance. He must have been under enormous pressure from the others, or else he would not have asked specifically "that I might be saved from the plan of the spies."

So why go to the ancestors for help? Why did Caleb not just ask God in the silence of his heart to give him strength to resist the "plan of the spies" and then, with God's help, make a good report? I think we can safely assume Caleb did so!

Have you ever had such a pressing need in your life that, while you did indeed pour out your heart

---

[6] Numbers 13:6.
[7] Genesis 17:8.

to God, you then also asked a friend to pray for you? That's where Caleb was that day. He knew that there were other people he could ask to pray for him who were just as concerned about the success of the Children of Israel as Caleb was—the Parents of Israel themselves. And Caleb is not asking them to pray for him because they are holy men. But they are parents who, as parents, love their children and their grandchildren and even love unconditionally, as parents, the generations they will never see.

Let's also recall that Caleb in that moment was a sojourner in a strange land he had never seen. And it would be natural to be afraid. But he knew his ancestor Abraham had followed God's call to leave his own country and travel to the Land that God would show him.[8] And so these ancestors also know the feelings of fear and apprehension that Caleb was experiencing.

How far removed was Caleb from the people buried in the Cave of Machpelah? If you piece together Caleb's genealogy from biblical sources, Caleb was the great-great-great-great grandson of

---

[8] Genesis 12:1.

Abraham.[9] Some people might consider that distant, but I don't. Let me explain just how close a great-great-great-great grandfather is by introducing you to someone very important to me.

My Abraham: Wright Massey

I was born and raised in Wisconsin. But that fact flows in part from the decision of a man long ago who, like Abraham, left his land and became a sojourner in a distant place.

In 1819, a man named Wright Massey was born in Hollingsworth, England. In 1848, he married

---

[9] Caleb's genealogy is quite complicated, but it can be reconstructed out of passages primarily from 1st Chronicles. Judah, the son of Jacob and grandson of Abraham, was the father of Perez (1 Chron 2:4). Perez was the father of Hezron (1 Chron 2:5). Hezron was the father of Jerahmeel, Ram, and Chelubai (1 Chron 2:9). The man named Chelubai here is the Caleb sent as a spy. We know this because a Caleb, brother of Jerahmeel, is also called the father of Achsah in 1 Chron 3:42 and 3:49. Caleb son of Jephunneh is also called the father of Achsah in Josh 15:17. So how can this one man be both the son of Hezron and the son of Jephunneh? We read in the Babylonian Talmud Tractate Sotah 11b: "The son of Hezron? He was the son of Jephunneh (**ypnh**; יפנה)! He was a son who turned (**panah**; פנה) from the plan of the spies." This passage interprets "Jephunneh" as a title honoring the fact that he rejected and "turned away" from the bad report the other spies gave to the Children of Israel.

Betty Warhurst. They left England and moved to America in 1855, eventually settling in Moscow, Wisconsin. Their first son Joseph was born that same year. Wright Jr. was born in 1858, followed by Edward in 1860, and finally Cornelius in 1864.

Wright Massey passed away in 1866 from "quick consumption" (probably Tuberculosis), leaving Betty to raise four young boys on her own. She did admirably and lived to see them all grown up and with families of their own when she passed on in 1900.

Their son Edward married Mary Diamond on January 2, 1882. Their first child, William, was born in December of that year. William married Rose Roethlisberger in 1906. Their son William Allan was born in 1912. William Allan married Helen Adler in 1935. Their second son, William Frederick, was born in 1939.

William Frederick Massey married Nancy Dodge in 1958. My twin brother Kevin and I are their third and fourth sons respectively, born in 1966.

And so, Wright Massey is my great-great-great grandfather. He is to me what the Patriarch Isaac was to Caleb. But Wright Massey was the Abraham to the large clan of Masseys descended from him here in the United States. He and Betty bravely came to America seeking a better life for themselves and the family they would have.

At the age of forty-seven, he lay on his death bed, leaving behind his dear wife Betty and four young sons, ages ten, eight, five, and two. He must have been so overwhelmingly concerned with their future safety and wellbeing. Wisconsin in 1866 was no easy place to eke out an existence. And he passed from this life, with a heart full of love and concern for them.

And where did that love go?

> Love is stronger than death (Song of Songs 8:6)

That love lived on in a soul that joined eternity, wishing health, happiness, and prosperity upon his children and his children's children whom he never met in life.

Wright Massey's son Edward died the same year my own father was born, which shows you that what may seem like multiple generations are not so very far apart. Edward's own son William, Wright's grandson, died one year *after* I was born and I have been told that he held his twin great-grandsons in his arms.

Which brings us back to the point. These people I have been describing care for me because I am one of them. Wright Massey knows me and wants what is best for me just as much as for those four boys he left behind.

I've described my ancestor Wright Massey as going into eternity with love and concern for the young children he left under the care of his beloved Betty. Can't we just assume our ancestors pray for us? Why do we have to *ask* them to "seek mercies" on our behalf?

One answer is, that's how relationships work. We may know in our heart of hearts that someone loves us, but it sure still feels good to hear it! If I never asked my ancestor to pray for me because I just assumed they were already doing it, I would not experience the communion of spirit that such a request can build between us. And it may even be that my ancestor, whose knowledge of me is solely dependent on the grace and power of God, cannot pray on my behalf *unless* I ask him.

There is obviously much we will simply never know on this side of eternity about the nature of the heavenly realm. What we *know with our minds* may be a collection of verses from the Bible about the matter. And I will get to all of those later in this book.

But another answer for why we need to ask them to pray for us, and I think it's the most important reason of all, is that the need to continue speaking with them is something *we feel in our hearts*. If you have lost a loved one, someone you frequently spoke with and cherished, you did not want that relationship to end. And yet death inevitably takes people from us. What I am saying is that death does not have to *end* that relationship. It changes it, to be sure.

But the very fact that we still want to talk to those people teaches us that we *should*. We have the promise in Scripture that our hearts are where we shall find God's law:

I will put my laws into their minds, and
write them on their hearts (Hebrews 8:10,
quoting Jeremiah 31:33)

In the New Covenant, Truth is instilled within
the hearts of the believers. Inside of Christian
history, asking the departed saints to pray for us
became a common and fully accepted practice.
And this fact alone gives us the assurance that
asking the departed to pray for us is within God's
Will.[10]

Praying for them and asking them to pray for
us is how our relationship with the dead continues.
Talk to your beloved dead. Ask them to "seek
mercies" on your behalf. Ask God to have mercy on
them. In so doing, we remain in relationship with
those whom we love, even after they pass into
eternity.

---

[10] I explore this concept in more detail in the Appendix.

But Isn't Saint Intercession Wrong??!!

If you come from a faith community that rejects and condemns the idea of asking the deceased to pray for us, perhaps you may want to skip right ahead to the Appendix of this book, entitled "Should You Ask the Dead to Pray for You?" There you will find a discussion of the verses of Scripture quoted by those who disagree with Saint or Ancestral Intercession. I will show you in the Appendix that Saint and Ancestral Intercession is supported by biblical evidence. Then, when you are more comfortable with asking the deceased to pray for us, you can better appreciate the further evidence in the next chapter that Ancestral Intercession was a common and accepted practice of earlier generations and should be still today.

But I repeat. Listen to your heart. If the love you feel for someone who has died prompts you to talk to them, why would you stifle that because someone quotes a Bible verse *they* say means you shouldn't be doing that?

If you are true to your heart and your conscience, you will continue speaking to your beloved dead unless they show you a place in the

Bible where it literally says "Thou shalt not speak` to your beloved dead. And the only things that are true are what's in the Bible." You'll find that what I just quoted is not, in fact, in the Bible at all! I explain all the verses they *will* quote you in the Appendix.

My Community is Fine with Saint Intercession, But I Want More Proof on Ancestral Intercession!

If you would like yet more evidence from Scripture and early Jewish and Christian writers that Ancestral Intercession was really practiced, continue to the next chapter. There I will describe New Testament proofs for the practice, as well as showing you passages from early Jewish and Christian writers which demonstrate an awareness and practice of Ancestral Intercession in the early centuries AD.

CHAPTER TWO:
THE SEARCH FOR
ANCESTRAL INTERCESSION

Ancestral Intercession
in the New Testament

As a Christian, I was primarily interested in exploring whether any possible echo of the practice of Ancestral Intercession was preserved in the New Testament itself. And so I expanded my search for terms such as "mercy" and the biblical Patriarchs to see what might emerge. I discovered that Jesus Himself tells a parable that describes Ancestral Intercession!

Recall the parable of the Rich Man and Lazarus in the Gospel of Luke. In this story, a certain Rich Man lived in great luxury, while a poor beggar named Lazarus was laid at the Rich Man's gate, hoping to eat whatever might fall from the Rich

Man's table. (And the parable never says he got so much as a crumb!)

> It happened that the poor man died and he was carried by the angels into the Bosom of Abraham. The Rich Man also died and was buried. (Luke 16:22)

Jesus then tells us that after the Rich Man had died and was in Hades, he saw Lazarus far away, in Abraham's bosom. He called out:

> **Father Abraham, have mercy on me**... (Luke 16:24)

Notice the amazing similarity between this simple prayer and what Caleb also reportedly prayed in the Talmud:

> Talmud: **My Fathers, seek mercy on my behalf**...
> Luke: **Father Abraham, have mercy on me**...

The Rich Man calls the Patriarch "Father Abraham" because he is appealing to him as one of Abraham's direct descendants. And just like Caleb, the Rich Man asks for "mercy."

Both passages include a petition immediately after asking for mercy:

> Talmud: My fathers, **seek mercy** on my behalf, **that I may be saved** from the plan of the spies.
>
> Luke: Father Abraham, **have mercy on me and send Lazarus** so that he may dip the tip of his finger in water and **cool my tongue**, because I am suffering in this fire. (Luke 16:22)

Now, despite the similarity between these passages, someone might protest that the Rich Man in this story has gone to Hades because of his lack of charity in life and therefore his example and prayer should be no model for us in the Church. But notice in the story itself, Abraham does not tell the Rich Man not to speak with him. Abraham does not tell the Rich Man that he should be praying directly to God and not asking him for mercy. That simply isn't the point of the story.

But there is another important aspect of this parable. Jesus presents the blessed afterlife as

involving communion and contact with the
Patriarch Abraham! Why has Jesus not instead
described Lazarus as resting in the blessed
presence of God?

Jesus is not denying in this story that our
ultimate destiny and hope is communion with our
loving God and Father. But He also describes it as
including communion with our human fathers. It
is not an "either-or." It's a "both-and."

And so, this parable describes communion and
contact with our Patriarch Abraham as an
essential component of a blessed afterlife. And if
such communion with our ancestors is important
in our afterlives, might it not be equally essential
while we still live and breathe?

This is not the only passage where Jesus
includes the biblical Patriarchs specifically in His
description of the end of time. Take note of the
following verse:

> I say to you, many will come from East and
> West **and they will recline (at table)
> with Abraham, Isaac, and Jacob in
> the Kingdom of Heaven**. (Matt 8:11)

The metaphor of a meal conveys communion and fellowship. And so Jesus once again here describes such fellowship **with the Patriarchs** as a component of a blessed afterlife.

St. Paul teaches us that gentiles who are not biologically descended from Abraham are his children through faith in Jesus:

> For you are children of God through faith in Christ. (Gal 3:26)
> If you are of Christ, then you are the offspring of Abraham, heirs according to the promise. (Gal 3:29)

And if anyone listening to Jesus thought they should not ask their ancestors, the biblical Patriarchs, to pray for them on the grounds that they were dead, Jesus Himself insists they are not dead at all, but alive in the presence of God:

> Have you not read that which was spoken to you by God, '**I am the God of Abraham, and the God of Isaac, and the God of Jacob**'? God is not the God of the dead, but **of the living**. (Matt 22:32)

Jesus depicted an example of Ancestral Intercession in one of His parables and He further describes communion with departed ancestors at the end of time. This made me wonder if any other evidence for Ancestral Intercession could be discovered in the Old Testament or early Jewish and Christian writers.

Ancestral Intercession in the Old Testament

The Old Testament itself does not present any case in which someone directly asks one of their departed ancestors for their prayer. This, of course, does not mean that people in the Old Testament period were *not* asking their beloved dead to pray for them. The story of Caleb preserved in the Talmud makes it possible that they were. But the Old Testament does still describe the importance of a spiritual relationship with Abraham, Isaac, and Jacob, as well as one's more immediate direct ancestors.

The first example of a prayer that invokes the name of an ancestor comes from one of the Patriarchs themselves:

And Jacob said, "**O God of my father Abraham, God of my father Isaac**, LORD, the one saying to me, 'Return to your land and to your relatives, and I will do good to you'." (Gen. 32:10)

Jacob is not, in his prayer, telling God something God doesn't already know. God knows He called Abraham and miraculously intervened for the birth of Isaac. And God knows that Isaac is Jacob's father. So when Jacob addresses God as the "God of my father Abraham, the God of my father Isaac," he is invoking their names as an appeal to his ancestors' merits before God. He is daring to remind God of the promises made to his ancestors that, through Abraham and his descendants, God would raise up a great people.

Appealing to the memory of the Patriarchs, and asking *God's mercy on behalf of them* is a way to remain spiritually connected to these dear ancestors.

My Fathers' Graves

We saw that Caleb asked his ancestors to pray for him while visiting their grave. Evidence of devotion to one's parents through their places of burial is also found in the Book of Nehemiah. Note the following exchange, when the Persian King Artaxerxes asked his cupbearer Nehemiah why he seemed sad:

> I said to the king, "May the king live forever! Why should my face not be sad, when the city, the house of **the graves of my fathers**, is in ruin, and its gates have been consumed by fire?"
> And the king said to me, "What are you asking for?"
> **And I prayed to the God of heaven**.
> And I said to the king:
> "If it is good to the king, and if your servant is good in your sight, that you send me to Judah, to the city of **the graves of my fathers**, and I will rebuild it."
> (Neh 2:3-5)

This passage from Nehemiah is an important lesson to us on the matter of how to prioritize our prayer life. He clearly shows concern for the graves of his ancestors here. But Nehemiah's first recourse in prayer **is directly to God Himself**. Asking others, whether living or deceased, to pray for us can and should be a component of our spiritual lives. But asking others to intercede for us would be meaningless if we were not first and foremost making our own prayers directly to God for assistance with our needs.

Ancestral Intercession in Early Jewish Writings

In my further searches on this topic I uncovered examples in early Jewish Literature where the Patriarchs are described as praying **for their children**.

The Jewish writer Philo of Alexandria (1st century AD, writing in Greek) tells us the Holy Patriarchs, Abraham, Isaac, and Jacob:

> Are not used to offering up powerless prayers **on behalf of their sons and daughters**, **because the Father has given to them, as a reward, that they**

will be heard in their prayers."[11]

Notice, the focus here is not their prayer as *saints*, but as *parents*, "**on behalf of their sons and daughters**."

Also, the early Jewish writing the Apocalypse of Zephaniah (1st or 2nd century AD, probably a Greek original surviving only in Coptic translation) states the following:

> We pray to you on account of those who are in all these torments so **that you might have mercy on all of them**."
> And when I saw them, I said to the Angel who spoke with me, ("Who are these?") He said, "**These who beseech the Lord are Abraham, Isaac, and Jacob**."[12]

---

[11] De Praemiis 166.
[12] Apocalypse of Zephaniah 11:1-4. P. 515, *Old Testament Pseudepigrapha*, edited by James H. Charlesworth.

Ancestral Intercession
in Early Christian Writings

St Cyril of Jerusalem (4th century AD) wrote a book entitled "The Mystogogical Catecheses," a description of Christian beliefs and practices for new converts. He writes about invoking Saints in the Christian service in the following way:

> Then we commemorate also those who have fallen asleep before us, **first Patriarchs**, Prophets, Apostles, Martyrs, **that by their prayers and intercessions** God would receive our petition.[13]

Notice that he describes the request for intercession as including "*first Patriarchs*." This preserves evidence that Ancestral Intercession specifically invoking the biblical Patriarchs was still alive in the early Church.

---

[13] Mystogogical Catecheses 23.9.

Ancestral Intercession
in Early Christian Inscriptions

Christian inscriptions found in catacombs and gravestones from the earliest centuries, a time when the Church was under persecution, show that the common piety of regular and faithful Christians included addressing their beloved dead and asking them to intercede in heaven on behalf of the living.

The inscriptions I will present are sometimes difficult to date with precision. But all these inscriptions date somewhere before the year AD 300. Consider the following example from the Cemetery of Priscilla in Rome.

> ZOSIME PAX TECVM
> Zosimus, Peace be with you.[14]

For as short and sweet as this inscription is, it is certainly an example of addressing the dead and praying for them. The Latin form of the name in the inscription ZOSIME is what is known as the vocative, in other words, it's the form of that name

---

[14] P. 76, *Christian Epigraphy*, by Orazio Marucchi (Cambridge University Press, 1912).

you use *when you are talking to that person.*

Here's yet another example from that location and very early time period:

> STAFILI PAX TECVM IN DEO HAVE VALE
> Stafilius, Peace be with you in God. Hail, Farewell.[15]

This inscription also uses the vocative form that proves the inscriber is indeed addressing the dead.

It is important to remember that, at the time these inscriptions were made, there were Christian leaders who oversaw these burials and would have had the right to approve or disallow the inscriptions that were carved there. If the Early Christian Church really did condemn any address to the dead, these inscriptions would simply not have happened!

Here's yet another example from the Cemetery of Priscilla in Rome:

---

[15] P. 84, *Christian Epigraphy.*

ΕΡΩΤΑ ΥΠΕΡ ΤΩΝ ΤΕΚΝΩΝ
Pray for your children[16]

This short inscription is an ancient example of early Christians practicing Ancestral Intercession!

The Inscription of Pectorius

A Christian epitaph, written in Greek, was found in 1839 in Autun, France. It dates to the 3rd century AD. In the inscription, a son prays for his mother and then asks his parents that they pray for him:

ΕΥ ΕΥΔΟΙ Μ[Η]ΤΗΡ ΣΕ ΛΙΤΑΖΟΜΕ ΦΩΣ
ΤΟ ΘΑΝΟΝΤΩΝ
ΑΣΧΑΝΔΙΕ [ΠΑ]ΤΕΡ ΤΩΜΩΙ
ΚΕ[ΧΑ]ΡΙΣΜΕΝΕ ΘΥΜΟΙ
ΣΥΝ ΜΗ[ΤΡΙ ΓΛΥΚΕΡΗΙ ΚΑΙ
ΑΔΕΛΦ]ΟΙΣΙΝ ΕΜΟΙΣΙΝ
Ι[ΧΘΥΟΣ ΕΙΡΗΝΙ ΣΟΥ] ΜΝΗΣΕΟ
ΠΕΚΤΟΡΙΟΙΟ

---

[16] P. 154, *Christian Epigraphy.*

May my mother sleep in peace, I beseech
thee, Light of the dead
Aschandius, my father, beloved of my heart,
with my sweet mother and my brethren be
mindful of thy Pectorius, abiding in the
peace of the Fish.[17]

Di Manes:
Ancient Roman Ancestral Intercession

Ancient Romans absorbed Greek culture and
religion, but they kept alive their own devotion to
their departed ancestors. Each home had a shrine
called a *lararium*, at which the head of the
household would lead prayers and sacrifices to the
family's departed ancestors. Ancient Roman
gravestones would include a prayer to the
ancestors using the Latin phrase *Dis Manibus*,
"For the ghost gods." This was put on gravestones
in the abbreviation D.M.

What is remarkable is that there are *Christian*
inscriptions from the earliest centuries that also
include the abbreviation D.M.[18] There would be no

---

[17] Pp. 21-22, *Christian Inscriptions*, by Henry Nunn (Society
for Promoting Christian Knowledge, 1920).

better way for an ancient Roman Christian, who regularly practices Ancestral Intercession, to express their devotion to their departed ancestors than to include D.M. on a gravestone. And there is no reason to believe that these early Christians excluded their pagan ancestors from this intercession. I personally think that ancient Greeks and Romans, who embraced Christianity, were baptized believing that they could then pray for the souls of their pagan ancestors while continuing to ask them to "seek mercies" on their behalf. This, in fact, is what St. Paul is referring to when he says that some "are baptized on behalf of the dead" (1 Cor 15:29).

And so we can certainly conclude from these early Christian inscriptions that the common piety of the Church in the very earliest period included addressing our own departed ancestors and asking them to pray for us.

---

[18] Pp. 99-100, *Christian Epigraphy.*

The Ancient and Current Status of Ancestral Intercession

I had certainly discovered evidence that some early Jews and Christians would have seen no problem in asking the earliest Patriarchs of our Faith, Abraham, Isaac, and Jacob, to pray for them. As well, there were those who asked their departed loved ones, their own fathers, mothers, grandparents, and great-grandparents to intercede for them.

But I was puzzled by a curious discrepancy. Rabbinic and other early Jewish literature knew of Ancestral Intercession, and yet the practice is not common or openly approved today in Judaism. And not just Ancestral Intercession, but any intercession directed at the deceased, including non-relative saints.

And yet, despite the reference I just quoted from St. Cyril of Jerusalem above, and the witness of early Christian inscriptions, the early Christian Church seemed to have discontinued the practice of Ancestral Intercession specifically, but amplified the practice of asking saints in general for their prayers. And in particular, the Christian

Church, both East and West, came to place particular emphasis on asking Mary, the Mother of Jesus, to pray for them.

Who was right? And who was wrong? And what should we be doing today?

In the next chapter I will explain what my research suggests happened to the practice of Ancestral Intercession in the early Jewish and Christian communities. It certainly faded into near oblivion in both the Jewish community and in the Christian West. But I will show that it survived in a sense in the Eastern Orthodox Church and so it can certainly come alive once again for all those interested in restoring it to their own spiritual lives.

In chapter four, I will explain how and why we today can and should reclaim the ancient prayer form of Ancestral Intercession. I will describe how I personally practice Ancestral Intercession and I will show you practical ways to incorporate it into your prayer life.

CHAPTER THREE:
WHAT HAPPENED TO ANCESTRAL INTERCESSION?

In this chapter, I will explore what happened historically that resulted in the practice of Ancestral Intercession being either forbidden or severely neglected in the Jewish and Christian communities. This has implications for what we can and should be doing today in our prayer lives.

Intercession from the Deceased in Judaism

The passages we explored in Chapter One—Caleb asking his ancestors to "seek mercies" on his behalf, people going to graveyards and asking their beloved dead to "seek mercies" on their behalf—these passages could never have been included in the Talmud if, when such Rabbinical Literature was being compiled, a request for prayer from deceased ancestors was universally condemned in the Jewish community. Even if some people did not practice Ancestral Intercession, enough of the community must still have performed it that a description of this prayer form could appear in the Babylonian Talmud.

As I researched this matter further, I found that my outsider perception that Judaism today universally condemns the practice of Saint Intercession was not at all accurate. A better description would be that it was condemned by *most* both within the Talmud and in Jewish history. But at the same time, advocates of Saint Intercession have continued to exist even to this day, especially in Kabbalist and Hasidic communities.[19] I will now survey for you some of the literature from ancient times that disapproves of the practice of Ancestral and Saint Intercession.

---

[19] See, for instance, *Holy Living: Saints and Saintliness in Judaism*, by Louis Jacobs, pp. 124-126.

Arguments Against Ancestral Intercession in the Talmud

Rabbinical Literature frequently contains contrary opinions on a matter. And so, not surprisingly, there are passages in the Talmud that argue against asking the dead for intercession. For instance, in the Babylonian Talmud, Berakhot 18a, there is an account of Rabbi Hiyya and Rabbi Jonathan walking in a cemetery. The blue fringe of Rabbi Jonathan was touching the ground. When Rabbi Hiyya told him that the dead might be insulted by this, Rabbi Jonathan said:

> **Do they know so much? Is it not written, But the dead do not know anything**?

The pertinent point here is a quote from the Book of Ecclesiastes:

> For the living know that they will die, **but the dead do not know anything, and there is no more reward for them. For their memory is lost**. Even their love, even their hate, even their envy have already perished. **And there is no more**

share for them forever in all that is done under the sun. (Ecclesiastes 9:5-6)

Now, this quote from Ecclesiastes is true only if *all* of it is true. This quote states that the dead not only know nothing, but they are utterly gone. They do not exist. Any Jew or Christian who believes that the dead await a reward cannot possibly quote Ecclesiastes 9:5-6 as proof that we can't ask the dead to pray for us, since this passage teaches that the very reason they know nothing is that, again, they don't exist. If they do await a reward, then they *still* exist. And if they still exist, it may be possible to ask them to pray for us.

Arguments Against Ancestral Intercession in Early Jewish Literature

Pseudo-Philo

An anonymous early Jewish writer explicitly condemns asking the deceased to pray for us. This writer's work is known as Pseudo-Philo and it dates somewhere between the first and third centuries AD. It was likely written in Hebrew but only a Latin translation survives to this day. In this book, the people ask the judge Deborah to pray for them after she passes away. Here is her response:

> While someone is yet living, he can pray for himself and for his sons. **But after his end, he will not be able to pray nor remember anyone**. (Pseudo-Philo 33.5)

The tone here suggests that the author of Pseudo Philo puts this argument in Deborah's mouth precisely because people in his community *are* asking the dead for prayer and he does not approve of the practice.

The Jerusalem Talmud condemns asking angels to pray for us in the following passage:

> If a person faces trouble, **let him not cry out to the angels Michael or Gabriel**. But he should cry out to me and I will immediately answer him. (Talmud Yerushalmi Berakhot 9:1)

Again, this passage of the Talmud would not exist unless people were, in fact, asking Michael and Gabriel and other angels to pray for them. And if they were asking angels for prayer they were possibly also asking deceased loved ones and other saints for prayer as well.

Maimonides' 13 Principles

The Medieval Jewish scholar Maimonides[20] formulated a creed of what constituted, in his opinion, the Jewish faith. These are known as the 13 Principles.[21] In number 5 of his list, Maimonides firmly rejects any address to angels or the dead. While written originally in Arabic, here is a Hebrew summary of this principle commonly included in prayer books:

> I believe with complete faith that to the Creator, may His Name be blessed, and to Him alone is it proper to pray, and it is not proper to pray to any other but Him.
>
> אני מאמין באמונה שלמה שהבורא יתברך שמו
> לו לבדו ראוי להתפלל ואין לזולתו ראוי להתפלל[22]

---

[20] Rabbi Moses Ben Maimon (Latinized to Maimonides) lived from AD 1135-1204. He is also known as RaMBaM, an acronym from **Rabbeinu Mosheh Ben Maimon**.
[21] He outlined these in his *Commentary on the Mishnah*, Tractate Sanhedrin 10.
[22] P. 61, The Book of Daily Prayers for Every Day of the Year (C. Sherman, 1848)

Maknisey-Raḥamim:
Angelic Intercession Survives in Judaism!

But, remarkably, despite the existence of a school of thought in Judaism that opposes addressing anyone but God in prayer, official prayers of Judaism, still recited to this day, contain explicit examples of asking the angels to pray for us.

Scattered throughout the *Seliḥot*, the penitential prayers of the Jewish High Holy Days, are prayers addressed directly to the angels, asking them to intercede on our behalf. The most famous of these is called, by its first words in Hebrew, the *Maknisey- Raḥamim*. The first line of this prayer reads as follows:

> (You Angels) Ushering in mercy
> (***raḥamim***), usher in our mercies before
> the Lord of mercy (***raḥamim***).
> מכניסי רחמים הכניסו רחמינו לפני בעל הרחמים

As you are now well acquainted with the idiom "seek mercies" (***raḥamim***), you are not at all surprised to see that the same word is used in this intercessory prayer.

Intercessory Prayer in Judaism

Prayers such as the ***Maknisey-Raḥamim*** are the exception that proves the rule. And the continued recitation of such prayers is a matter of controversy within Judaism.[23] The position of Maimonides generally won out in normative Jewish practice, with the result that Saint or Ancestral Intercession is not encouraged within Judaism.

The fact that the ***Maknisey-Raḥamim*** ever existed, let alone continued to be prayed publicly, is an echo of a past time when asking the angels and our beloved deceased to "seek mercies on our behalf" was indeed a part of popular piety.[24]

---

[23] For a detailed description of the historical Jewish debate on the topic, read "Between Worldliness and Traditionalism: Eighteenth-Century Jews Debate Intercessory Prayer" by David Malkiel (*Jewish Studies, an Internet Journal* 2 [2003], pp. 169-198: http://www.biu.ac.il/JS/JSIJ/2-2003/Malkiel.pdf)

[24] For an excellent survey of how common Jewish Intercessory Prayer during the Talmudic period was, see "Prayers of Jews to Angels and Other Intermediaries during the First Centuries CE" by Professor Meir Bar-Ilan (*Saints and Role Models in Judaism and Christianity*, pp. 79-95).

Ancestral Intercession in Early Christianity

As St. Cyril of Jerusalem attests, early Christian liturgy still included intercession to the biblical Patriarchs as an important spiritual component. And we saw Christian inscriptions which included examples of prayers asking our ancestors to pray for us. And yet, if you asked Christians today about the practice of Ancestral Intercession, they would not understand what you were talking about. And as I described above, it faded away in Jewish practice because the school of thought which strongly fought against it largely won out in that community.

But the practice of asking the *Saints* to pray for us **thrived** in the Christian Church. Protestant Reformers argued against Saint Intercession starting in the 15th century AD, but it was accepted throughout the Christian Church prior to that point.

If Saint Intercession did so well in the Church, why did Ancestral Intercession specifically decline in the Christian Church?

The answer will be, it actually didn't. In the Eastern Orthodox Church it never *entirely* vanished. But in both the Eastern and Western Church it evolved by a natural and understandable development into a new focus. And that doesn't mean that we shouldn't return to regularly asking our ancestors to pray for us. Let's explore what happened to Ancestral Intercession in Christianity and learn the implications for what our current practice can and should be today.

Veneration of Old Testament Saints in the Eastern Orthodox Church

I was born on June 15. My Romanian wife informed me that a friend back in her home country had commissioned the painting of an icon for my birthday. When the friend gifted me with the item, I was puzzled. It was an icon of "St. Amos," whose "Saint Day" on the Eastern Calendar is June 15. As a former Protestant, I was, of course, very familiar with the *Prophet* Amos of the Old Testament. But I was confused by how an Old Testament figure could be considered a *Saint*.

That was my first exposure to the fact that the Eastern Orthodox Church continues to venerate Old Testament Patriarchs, Prophets, and other worthies right alongside Christian martyrs and saints.

The Eastern Orthodox Church commemorates all the Holy Forefathers, from Adam and Eve, through Abraham and Sarah, down through David, and up to Mary the Mother of Jesus on the 2nd Sunday before Christmas.

A hymn sung on that day shows the Eastern Orthodox Church's continued understanding of those ancestors as interceding for mercy on our behalf:

> Through Faith You justified the Forefathers, betrothing through them the Church of the Gentiles.
> These saints exult in glory, for from their seed has come forth a glorious fruit:
> She who bore You without seed.
> So **by their prayers**, O Christ God, **have mercy on us!**

The Patriarch Abraham is venerated in the Eastern Orthodox Church on October 9. Here is a song in honor of Abraham which is sung on that day:

> You were the servant, a mortal fashioned from the earth; your master was God, the Lord and Fashioner of Creation. And yet, well pleased to glorify your greatness in Heaven, the Lord of All has called Himself "The God of Abraham." **Procure for us mercies** from your **merciful** Lord.

The final line of this hymn is virtually the same thought as the prayer of Caleb at the Cave of Machpelah! It is startling to find that the Eastern Orthodox Church has so perfectly preserved the knowledge that Ancestral Intercession should include an appeal that the Patriarch **seek mercy on our behalf**.

So, in fact, the Eastern Orthodox Church never abolished the practice of asking the Patriarchs to intercede mercies upon us. Indeed, the Church never stopped doing so in her official liturgies.

The Western Church, which became the Roman Catholic Church and the various Protestant Churches that later broke away from the Catholics, did not preserve any active sense of communication or communion with the Old Testament Patriarchs or Prophets. Certainly people in the West read their Bibles, but that did not mean they viewed Abraham, Isaac, and Jacob as saints worthy of public veneration, let alone intercession.

But even if the Eastern Orthodox Church preserved an echo of the lost practice of Ancestral Intercession in her liturgies, continuing to venerate the biblical Patriarchs, the regular practice of asking our deceased parents to pray for us faded away in the Eastern Orthodox Church as well.

So what caused the fading of Ancestral Intercession which once existed in the Early Christian Church? I will suggest that two factors contributed to the decline.

1) The Rise of "Official" Saints

The word "saint" in the earliest Church referred to living Christians. [25] Over time, the title "Saint" was reserved more and more to people who had been officially declared by the Church to be glorified and in the presence of God. The liturgies of the Church asked only *these* Saints to pray for us. And people likely began to feel uncomfortable with asking their parents and grandparents, who were not official Saints, to pray for them.

Even so, there was never any Church teaching that asking a "non-official" saint to pray for you was wrong. Indeed, the process of declaring someone an official saint involves, in the Western Church, confirmed miracles that came from the deceased person's intercession, even before they are declared a "Saint." But people focused their intercessory energy on those departed heroes who seemed to have a chance of achieving such official recognized Sainthood. And, as a result, true and pure *Ancestral* Intercession faded away in the

---

[25] For instance, we read in 2 Corinthians 1:1, "Paul, an Apostle of Christ Jesus by the will of God, and Timothy our brother, to the church of God that is in Corinth, **with all the saints** throughout Achaia.

Christian Church.

I will say this, however. Ancestral Intercession never really ended because people, missing their loved ones, kept speaking with them. But in this book I am asserting that they not only should do it, but they should ask their ancestors to pray for them with boldness and openness and frequency.

Practicing Ancestral Intercession means regularly asking our ancestors, those we met in life and also those ancestors of older times, to pray for us because we know they love us and want what is best for us. And we should do this believing that each of us personally have no better prayer warriors than our actual direct ancestors who love us and want us to thrive.

2) Mary Eclipsed Abraham and the Other Ancestors

The second reason Ancestral Intercession faded away in Christianity is that, alongside the rise in devotion to "official" saints, the Virgin Mary achieved particular prominence. And as people lost touch with Ancestral Intercession, asking

Mary to pray for us was a natural replacement, since she was, indeed, a mother figure.

Abraham was the "friend" of God.[26] And he could boldly intercede with God, as we see in the account of how he asked God to spare the people of Sodom and Gomorrah if only a few righteous people were found there.[27]

But Mary is the "Mother" of God

When we call Mary the Mother of God, we are not so much honoring her as we are declaring the reality and the truth that the Son whom she bore was, while in her womb, fully human and fully divine. She was not the mother only of the human part of Him, because He was both human and divine, joined inseparably in one person.

Mary is Honored in Holy Scripture

Let us not forget that she herself declared in Holy Scripture that:

---

[26] Isaiah 41:8; James 2:23.
[27] Genesis 18:16-33.

Henceforth all generations will call me blessed. (Luke 1:48)

When Mary arrived at the house of her kinswoman Elizabeth, we read the following.

> It happened as Elizabeth heard **the greeting of Mary, the babe leaped in her womb**; and Elizabeth was filled with the Holy Spirit and she exclaimed with a loud voice, "**Blessed are you among women**, and blessed is the fruit of your womb! And why is this granted to me, **that the mother of my Lord should come to me**?" (Luke 1:41-43)

Some people read this passage and pretend that it was the unborn Jesus that caused this reaction in Elizabeth. The Bible makes it very clear, it was Mary herself. The babe in the womb of Elizabeth leaped when he heard the **greeting of Mary**. Elizabeth, filled with the Holy Spirit, declares **not**:

> Why is this granted to me that my Lord should come to me?

Rather she asks:

> Why is this granted to me, that the **mother of my Lord** should come to me?

The importance of Mary is also on full display in the account of the Wedding of Cana (John 2:1-11). Jesus and His disciples are at a wedding at which the wine has run out. Jesus' mother is also there, and tells Him, simply, "They have no wine."

He certainly understands that she is asking Him to intervene and solve this problem for them. And her request implies her knowledge of His ability to perform a miracle.

Traditional translations of Jesus' response to her make it sound like He takes an insulting tone with His Mother:

> "O Woman, what have you to do with me?" (John 2:4; RSV translation)

For reference, here is the original Greek of that statement:

ti emoi kai soi gynai?
τι εμοι και σοι γυναι?
Literally, "What to me and to you,
Woman?"

Other passages of the Bible make it clear that
nothing about Jesus' response insults or
denigrates His mother. It is certainly not true that
calling her "Woman" was an insult, since that is
how He addresses her from the cross, while
arranging for her protection:

> Therefore Jesus, seeing His mother and the
> disciple whom He loved standing near, He
> said to His mother, "**Woman (*gynai*;
> γυναι**), behold your son!" Then He said to
> the disciple, "Behold, your mother!" (John
> 19:26-27)

Far from insulting His Mother at the Wedding
at Cana, Jesus' words imply that He is subservient
to her will in this matter. The words He used to
state "What have you to do with me?" (*ti emoi
kai soi*) are identical to those spoken by a demon
in the Gospel of Mark 5:7, who was begging Jesus
from a position of subservience:

Jesus: What to me and to you (***ti emoi kai soi***), Woman?
Demon: What to me and to you (***ti emoi kai soi***), Jesus, Son of the Most High God?

The demon spoke these words and then begged for terms. He begged to be sent into a herd of pigs. Jesus spoke these words and then immediately worked a miracle in response to His mother's request.

Hail Mary, the Daughter of Abraham

The earliest Christian Church continued to ask Old Testament worthies to pray for them. But the earliest Christians also understood that, in Mary, the Church had an intercessor whose power before God eclipsed that of Abraham and the others.

One of the oldest recorded Christian hymns about Mary is found in the *Odes of Solomon*, a late 1st Century AD collection of poems written in the Syriac language. This song, written near the end of the Apostolic age, describes Mary as follows:

She conceived and gave birth. And the

Virgin became a Mother **with great mercies (*raḥme sagi'e*)**[28] (Odes of Solomon 19:6-7)

Notice the association now of Mary with the ***mercies*** people also asked Abraham to seek on their behalf.

Mary eclipsed Abraham because her place at the conclusion of Salvation History had clearly fulfilled the promises made to him at the beginning. In addition to both of them being intercessors in Scripture—Abraham for Sodom and Gomorrah and Mary for the Wedding Party—they also share a more important similarity. Both Abraham and Mary received their sons through miraculous births.

Abraham was told:

Is there anything too difficult for the LORD? At the appointed time I will return to you, at this time next year, and Sarah will have a son. (Gen 18:14)

---

[28] The word ***raḥme*** is the Syriac equivalent of the Hebrew word ***raḥamim.***

Mary was told:

For nothing will be impossible with God. (Luke 1:37)

And just as Abraham was willing to freely offer his only son,[29] Mary stood at the cross and did watch her only son freely sacrifice Himself for our sins.[30]

Ancestral Intercession: Yours to Reclaim Today

Ancestral Intercession was never entirely gone from Christian practice. The Eastern Orthodox Church even today formally recognizes Abraham and the other Patriarchs as saints. The Orthodox hymn to Abraham, sung on his Feast Day, even includes the precise request **that he intercede mercy for us,** which we saw in the story of Caleb from the Talmud.

The focus on Mary was probably even as a result of people's sense that she was not so much a

---

[29] Genesis 22:1-19.
[30] John 19:25-27.

saint, as our *mother*. People's desire to ask their ancestors to pray for them was perhaps funneled toward Mary, which the Church had sanctioned. But it never had to be just one or the other.

If intercession to our own beloved dead declined in Christian history alongside a growth in attention paid to the Virgin Mary and other "official" saints, that does not mean that Christians today cannot return to a regular practice of asking our deceased ancestors to pray for us.

The biblical Patriarchs and other Old Testament worthies, New Testament and other Christian saints, and especially our own immediate ancestors remain a valid recourse for intercessory prayer. That said, Christians today should also not cut themselves off from the legitimate role of our Matriarch Mary.

Mary herself describes her place in the Salvation History begun with Abraham:

> For the Mighty One has done great things for me and Holy is His Name. **His mercy** is to generation of generations to those fearing Him ... He has helped Israel his

servant, *in remembrance of His mercies*, just as He spoke to our fathers, to **Abraham** and to his seed forever.
(Luke 1:49-50, 54-55)

Jesus Himself informs us that:

Abraham your father leaped for joy that he might see my day; and he saw it and rejoiced. (John 8:56)

What Abraham saw and rejoiced at was the totality of the Gospel story. One of his own daughters declared "Behold, I am the handmaid of the Lord; let it be done to me according to your word." (Luke 1:38) And, by her obedience, she brought about the fulfillment of the promise God had made to him centuries earlier, that "by you all the families of the earth shall be blessed." (Gen 12:3)

What a blessing God has given us through Ancestral Intercession! In our heart of hearts we know that our loved ones who have passed away are still somehow there. When we speak to them, we feel close to them and that means, by the power of God, they have indeed heard us. And asking them to "seek mercies" on our behalf is soothing to our souls. Praying for them is yet another way we express our love for them. And so it is that, through prayer, our relationships with those beloved ancestors never really end.

CHAPTER FOUR:
THE PRACTICE AND BENEFITS OF ANCESTRAL INTERCESSION

In this chapter I will share how I personally incorporate Ancestral Intercession into my prayer life. While the practice itself is relatively simple, there are sound biblical and historical guidelines which govern how this practice should fit into a wider sense of spirituality. I will describe these issues and also show the Bible's general teachings on the subject of prayer.

Why Practice Ancestral Intercession?

Again, we ask our departed ancestors to pray for us because they love us. Their intercession *as parents* will result in a multiplication of prayers for us, their children.

The Bible gives us several examples of how the prayer of a parent on behalf of their child is readily heard by God:

> One of the synagogue leaders, Jairus by name, came, and seeing Jesus, he fell at His feet. **He begged Him much, "My daughter is at the last end**. Please come and put your hands on her so that she will be healed and live." **And Jesus went with him**. (Mark 5:22-24)

In 2 Kings 2:18-37, we also read about the Shunammite woman, whose son had suddenly died. **She implored the prophet Elisha for help**. And the prophet prayed to the LORD **and the boy was raised from the dead**.

We also read in Matthew 15:21-28 a wonderful account of how a woman persistently prayed on behalf of her daughter. A Canaanite woman came to Jesus. She cried out:

> **Have mercy on me, O Lord**, Son of David; **my daughter is badly demon possessed**.

Jesus did not reply. His disciples said:

Send her away, for she is crying after us.

So Jesus told her:

I was only sent to the lost sheep of the
house of Israel.
But she came and knelt before Him, saying
"Lord, help me."
He answered, "It is not good to take the
children's bread and throw it to the dogs."
She said, "Yes, Lord, yet even the dogs eat
the crumbs that fall from the table of their
masters."
Then Jesus answered her, "O woman, great
is your faith! Let it be done for you as you
wish.
**And her daughter was healed from
that very hour.**

How to Practice Ancestral Intercession

The most important thing to do if you would
like to practice Ancestral Intercession is, unless
you are already doing so, start praying to God.

Unless you are already firmly grounded in regular prayer directly to God, asking your own ancestors or any other saint to pray for you will be meaningless.

Here's why. We have many scriptural promises that God will answer our prayers when *we* ask them sincerely and persistently. And I will explain all the verses that describe these promises. But if we want anything through prayer, ***we have to pray to God***! If we ourselves do not ask God for something in prayer, there is no reason to believe that asking your father, or Abraham, or the Virgin Mary to pray for you will mean anything!

If you already have a discipline of prayer directly to God, excellent. If you don't, there's no time like the present to get started! I will now present some of the how's and why's of prayer, before returning to the way I personally incorporate requests for prayer from my ancestors into my prayer life.

Prayer 101: First the Good News!

The Good News is simple. God knows we are
sinful, weak, and scattered. And so, He accepts our
most meager effort in prayer. What Bible verse
proves this assertion?

Read the following, from St. Paul's Letter to the
Romans 8:26:

> Likewise also the Spirit helps our
> weaknesses; for **we do not know how to
> pray as we ought,** but **the Spirit
> Himself intercedes for us with sighs
> that cannot be spoken**.

We can take away from this verse that all we
have to do is try to pray to our Loving God and His
own Life-Giving Spirit will make up for our
insufficiency!

Thanks be to God that He blesses our humblest
efforts to draw near to Him. But the Bible also
gives us practical and straightforward advice and
guidance on the reasons and the manner in which
we should pray.

Why Should We Pray?

We should pray for the simple fact that the Bible clearly teaches us that God wills it. And the reason He wills it is that there are things He would give us, but only after we have prayed with persistence.

Why would God order His Universe in that way? Because it is understandable that He would want to reward those most faithful to Him with His blessings!

What verses prove my assertion that He wills us to pray and that there are things He would give us, but only after we have prayed with persistence?

God Wants Us To Pray

Jesus tells His disciples:

When you pray... (Matt 6:5, 6:6)

Notice, He does not say "If you pray."

Jesus implies that we are indeed to pray! He only wants to make sure we know how to do it when we perform this crucial practice.

God Wants Us To Pray With Persistence

But what about God only giving us things after we have prayed with persistence?

Jesus tells His disciples the following parable in the Gospel of St. Luke 18:1-7:

> Then He told them a parable to show them **that they should always pray and not give up**. He said: "In a certain town there was a judge who neither feared God nor respected man. And there was a widow in that town **and she came to him saying**, '**Grant me justice** against my adversary'. "For some time he refused. But finally he said to himself, 'Even though I don't fear God or respect man, yet **because this widow keeps troubling me, I will give her justice**, so that, coming in the end, she may not subdue me!'"

And the Lord said, "Listen to what the unjust judge says. And **will not God execute justice for his chosen ones, who cry out to him day and night**?"

Jesus also describes the need to be persistent in prayer in St. Luke 11:5-8. Immediately after teaching His Disciples the Lord's Prayer, Jesus tells the Parable of the Friend at Night:

He said to them, "Which of you, if you go to a friend at midnight, and say to him, 'Friend, lend me three loaves of bread, for a friend of mine has come to me from a journey, and I have nothing to set before him,' and he from within will answer and say, 'Don't trouble me. The door is now shut, and my children are with me in bed. I cannot get up and give it to you'? I tell you, even though he will not rise and give it to him because he is his friend, yet **because of his persistence, he will get up and give him as many as he needs**."

Jesus implies here that, even though someone is not inclined to grant a favor, they will do so merely to end the inconvenience of the situation.

Amazingly, Jesus then tells us that it's the same with God! Here's how He continues:

> So I say to you: Ask and it will be given to you; seek and you will find; knock and the door will be opened to you. For everyone who asks receives; the one who seeks finds; and to the one who knocks, the door will be opened. (Luke 11:9-10)

The implication here is that God will not freely give to us that for which we do not at least ask. We will not readily find that for which we do not seek!

God wants us to draw near to Him in prayer. And He wants to give us all that we truly need. We would never deepen our communion with Him if He gave us every dream and desire of our hearts without so much as us asking. And that is why He makes prayer the vehicle for receiving the benefits we believe we need.

It remains true that we will not receive everything for which we pray. And that is for the simple fact that God knows what truly is best for us. As Jesus continued the passage we were just reading from the Gospel of Luke, He tells us:

> What father among you, if his son asks for a
> fish, will instead of a fish give him a
> serpent; or if he asks for an egg, will give
> him a scorpion? (Luke 11:11-12)

Our Heavenly Father will only give us those things that are truly unto our good and unto our Salvation. If I ask God for what I think is a fish, but He knows it's actually a serpent, He won't "answer" that prayer. And that is why we may be confident that prayer which is ultimately unanswered, meaning not granted exactly as we wanted it, was all for the best in the end.

For What Should We Pray?

The answer in the Bible is simple. Ask from God in prayer everything that you reasonably can expect Him to want to give you.

Let's be honest, if you committed murder, you should not expect God to grant a prayer that you get away with it! No prayer asking for assistance to thrive or survive outside the boundaries of the Ten Commandments will be heard or granted.

But we can and should freely ask God for good health, protection from our enemies, strength to cope with our daily labors, guidance in our lives, and the blessings of prosperity in our livelihoods.

What verses prove these assertions? St. Paul writes:

> Be anxious about nothing, but in everything by prayer and supplication with thanksgivings **let your requests be made known to God**. (Phil 4:6)

Ask God for things! But ask God for things knowing that He knows what we really need and don't.

How Should We Pray?

Jesus gives us practical advice on this point in the Gospel of St. Matthew:

> And when you pray, do not be like the hypocrites, for they love standing to pray in the synagogues and in the open streets to be

seen by others. Truly I tell you, they have received their reward. (Matt 6:5)

In other words, any prayer we offer that is merely for appearance before other people, is not prayer at all. Jesus continues:

But when you pray, go into your room, close the door and pray to your Father in secret. Then your Father, who sees what is in secret, will reward you in the open. (Matt 6:6)

In other words, personal prayer must be a matter between you and God alone. Pray at times and in places where you certainly are not doing it merely for show. Jesus also implies here that prayer should be solitary. I personally like to pray when I am driving to work. Certainly no one can see that I am praying. That is, for me, sweet time alone with my Creator.

We also read in Ecclesiastes 5:2 that we should not think we will sway God with many words in prayer:

For God is in Heaven and you are on the Earth. Therefore let your words be few.

Jesus gives us excellent and practical advice in this same vein:

> And when you pray, do not babble like the heathen, for they think they will be heard because of their many words. Do not be like them, for **your Father knows what you need before you ask Him**. (Matt 6:7-8)

In other words, there is no point in making your prayer to God include any literary merit, fanciful adjectives, or the like. I mean, you're talking to the Creator of the Universe! You're not going to sway Him by rhetoric to grant you anything.

In fact, notice that Jesus tells us, "your Father knows what you *need* before you ask Him."

Jesus is telling us that we may indeed ask for things that our Father knows **we do not need**. But we should not expect Him to grant us anything we do not need and which is not unto our Salvation.

Thy Will Be Done

The fact that Jesus included the line "Thy Kingdom Come, **Thy Will be Done**" (Matt 6:10) in the Lord's Prayer is an important instruction that we should always pray fully submitted to God's Will for our lives. When I pray, I always include a prayer for strength and wisdom to accept God's Will. And I tell Him that I accept that whatever I ask and do not receive must be something that was not within His Will. I accept that my petitions, however important to me, are not necessarily what God knows is best for me.

When Should We Pray?

As for when we should pray, you will frequently see 1 Thessalonians 5:17 quoted:

> Pray without ceasing. (*adialeiptos proseuchesthe*; αδιαλειπτως προσευχεσθε)

Some commentators try to describe this passage as implying that we are somehow supposed to spend our lives in a constant state of prayer. But let's be honest. That's not reasonable and it can't possibly be what the verse is saying. God knows there are times when our minds must be fixated on some task and we will not be actively in prayer.

The word in question here, translated as "without ceasing" (***adialeiptos***), is used by St. Paul elsewhere in his letters. And the context makes it clear that the word does not mean "constantly and with no pause."

For instance, he tells the Romans:

> Without ceasing (***adialeiptos***) I mention you always in my prayers. (Rom 1:9)

Would this then mean that he never prays for the Christians in Galatia, Corinth, and Jerusalem? Clearly not.

The word translated as "without ceasing" (***adialeiptos***) simply means "without a significant pause." In other words, frequently and a lot.

So when should we pray? Whenever we can!

When our lives afford us time of solitude, we should pray. But Jesus also taught us, by example, that we should plan times in our lives to take ourselves out of the chaos of this world and find some time and place to be with our God:

> But He (Jesus) was withdrawing into the desert and was praying. (Luke 5:16)

Prayer Times in the Early Church

One of the oldest early Christian books apart from the New Testament is known as the *Didache*, the *Teaching of the Apostles*. Scholars believe it dates to the late 1st century, so it was written in a time when the last of the Apostles were passing on and the first generation of early Christians were spreading the Good News in the Roman Empire and beyond. And the *Didache* gives practical advice on how and when to pray. It tells us to pray the Lord's Prayer three times every day.[31] It does not specify prayer times, but it would be reasonable to assume that praying the Lord's Prayer three times a day would mean to pray it in

---

[31] *Didache* 8.

the morning, sometime around noon and again before going to sleep. As the Psalmist says:

> Evening, Morning, and at Noon I complain and murmur and He hears my voice. (Psalm 55:17)

Amen - I Believe

Prayers in the Judeo-Christian tradition frequently end with the Hebrew word **Amen** (אמן), which means "truly," "it is so." It is quite proper to close our prayers with this word, because we have been taught in Scripture that it is important to actively believe we will receive that for which we pray:

> Whatever you ask in prayer, **believe that you have received it** and it will be yours. (Mark 11:24)

> **If you have faith as a grain of mustard seed**, you will say to this mountain, "Move from here to there," and it will move. And nothing will be impossible for you. (Matt 17:20-21)

The word **Amen** is a way to pause for a moment and gather our faith and trust in God that, if our petition is within His Will, we will receive that for which we ask.

And On To the Ancestors!

Alright, so you've got a regular discipline of praying directly to our loving God and Father. You ask Him for things in prayer. And now there is no reason not to also ask others to pray for you and your needs. And there are no better prayer warriors waiting to come to your assistance than your spiritual and physical ancestors, who love you and want all the best for you.

I will now describe to you my overall prayer discipline and how it incorporates Ancestral Intercession. I certainly do not present my practice as in any way implying that this is the one way people ought to pray.

Prayer is not a magic formula we recite to have God grant us all our wishes. I take great comfort in Romans 8:26 which I quoted above, that the God knows we do not know how to pray as we ought. I trust that the Holy Spirit takes whatever stumbling and bumbling words I make and turns them into acceptable prayer. I describe this to you merely as a way to show how one might combine prayer to God and a request for prayer from one's ancestors.

Keith's Prayer Regimen

First, I make the Sign of the Cross and I say, "In the Name of the Father, and of the Son, and of the Holy Spirit" (Matthew 28:19).

I first pray to God in thanksgiving for all the many blessings He has given me. This grounds me in the fact that I really do look back and realize all the ways God has been with me in times of trouble and strengthened me in my trials. When I compare my life to those of others around the world who suffer horrible hardships, it humbles me and puts the petitions I will eventually make into perspective. Whatever I may ask of God, I give Him thanks for all He has already given and would continue to cheerfully do so even if, in His Will, He will not be granting me my petitions exactly as I might seek.

Then I pray the Our Father. Now, my main prayer time is in the morning during my commute to work (I teach Latin at a public high school). I drink my coffee and listen to news for the first several minutes. When the coffee is finished, I turn off the radio and head into my morning prayers. As I described above, the earliest Church taught the discipline of praying the Our Father three times a day. So, I include it in my morning prayers, with the intention then of praying it twice more, close to noon and again in the evening. I'm going to be honest with you. I sometimes find myself at the end of my day reflecting and realizing that I didn't get to those other prayer times. When that happens, I pray the Our Father one more time and trust that my loving God and Father knows my weakness and accepts my efforts. I certainly don't pray the Our Father twice in a row just to make it three for the day, because prayer is not a magic formula.

After the Our Father, I pray the ancient prayer known as the Trisagion (Thrice Holy). It goes like this:

Holy God, Holy Mighty, Holy Immortal,
have mercy on us.
Holy God, Holy Mighty, Holy Immortal,
have mercy on us.
Holy God, Holy Mighty, Holy Immortal,
have mercy on us.
Glory be to the Father, and to the Son, and
the Holy Spirit, now and ever and unto ages
of ages, Amen.
Holy and Immortal, have mercy on us.
Holy God, Holy Mighty, Holy Immortal,
have mercy on us.

Now, if you weren't raised in a liturgical
tradition, you might wonder why a prayer should
include repetition such as the Trisagion does. I
mean, God surely heard us the first time, right?
Why repeat anything?

Keep in mind that repetition is quite biblical!
Take a look at Psalm 136:1-2:

O give thanks to the Lord for He is good,
**for His steadfast love endures
forever**.
O give thanks to the God of gods, **for His
steadfast love endures forever**.

And, if you know your Bible, you know this is not the end of it. The phrase "for His steadfast love endures forever" will be repeated a total of twenty-six times in this Psalm!

Praying with persistence *implies* that we will pray with repetition! Once, when Jesus was approaching Jericho, a blind man heard the crowd and asked what was going on. When he learned that Jesus of Nazareth was passing by, he cried out:

> Jesus, Son of David, have mercy on me! (Luke 18:38)

But people rebuked him and told him to be quiet. And he cried out again, repeating his original prayer:

> Son of David, have mercy on me! (Luke 18:39)

Only then did Jesus stop, ask him what he wanted, and heal him of his blindness. He would not have been healed if he had not simply repeated his prayer!

Now, there is a very important reason why I include this ancient prayer, asking for mercy, in my regimen. When I get to the time in which I will be asking my ancestors to "seek mercies on my behalf," I need to have asked God for mercy myself. Again, I cannot ask anyone to seek something on my behalf that I do not first and foremost ask myself from our God.

Before I ask God for specific things, I first pray that He grant me nothing that is not unto my salvation and for the grace to accept that His will may not include me receiving that for which I ask.

What do I pray for? Firstly, for good health. And I hope and pray that if I may have only one of my many petitions, that it would be good health!

It is reasonable for all of us to ask God for success in our vocations and our ventures. I ask for His protection, blessings, strength, and guidance in my job and my various other revenue projects. As a writer of non-fiction books and also fiction novels, I of course want to be seeing regular sales of those works. And so I pray to God that He both grant me sales each day and also that He guide me in practical matters of promotion to achieve such sales.

Again, I ask God for those things fully submitted to His Will. If measurable progress and success is not visible to me on any given day, I am not discouraged. I pray with persistence because I believe God wants me to. And whatever I have asked, in faith, from my God and not received, I trust that God has only given me what is in my best interest. It may be that He does intend to grant me that for which I ask, but not just yet. My personal and spiritual growth may require me to work through a length of time in which I patiently wait and continue to ask.

After I have made my various petitions I enter into a time of just free conversation with God. I may pour out my heart to Him, just vent frustrations about my job and other aspects of my life. Such time is itself a type of prayer. And it just feels good to tell my troubles to someone I know is really listening.

I then shift my prayer time toward asking my own beloved dead to pray for me. But before I go there, I first pray for them.

I pray for my late parents, my late grandparents, great-grandparents, aunts and uncles and cousins who have fallen asleep in the Lord. I use traditional Eastern Orthodox prayers for them, asking God to:

> Grant them rest in a Place of Brightness, a Place of Verdure, a Place of Repose.

And I especially pray **that God grant them mercy**. I pray for each of them by name **that God would grant them mercy**.

And this is also especially important. Because I will yet be asking them to "seek mercy on my behalf." I can't ask them to do anything for me that I have not done already for them!

> **Give and it will be given to you**; good measure, pressed down, shaken together, running over, will be put into your lap. **For by the same measure you give it will be measured back to you**. (Luke 6:38)

Ancestral Intercession in Practice

Now, God already has heard my petitions before I ask my ancestors to pray for me, to seek mercies on my behalf. The examples we saw above from the Talmud and the Gospel of Luke did indeed include a specific prayer request after asking the Patriarchs to seek mercies. I personally do not think enumerating all the details of my petitions again would be necessary or spiritually helpful. So I ask in general, that God would grant me my petitions, since He already knows what they are. I suppose if one had a particular pressing need, there would be nothing wrong with including it in a request for prayer to one's ancestors or other saints.

And so, as I ask my personal ancestors to pray for me, I simply ask, for example:

> Mom, pray for me, that God would grant me my petitions.

One could also use the same formula as Caleb and say instead "Seek mercies on my behalf." I repeat this for all of my beloved dead, my father, grandparents, great-grandparents, uncles, aunts, and cousins. And again, keep in mind, I have also prayed that God would grant them mercy.

The reason Ancestral Intercession is so soothing to the soul is that it is a way to have a relationship with our departed family members. We pray for them, asking God to have mercy on their souls. We ask them to pray for us, that they seek mercy on our behalf. It is indeed different from asking some Saint we've never met to pray for us. And there's nothing wrong with Saint Intercession. But Ancestral Intercession, asking our own loved ones to pray for us, even loved ones we've never met, such as Wright Massey is to me, is a comforting practice. And we can have confidence that our ancestors will intercede for us with all the love a parent has for a child.

I then do ask a number of "official" saints, who have meaning to me, for their intercession. My middle name is Andrew and I ask St. Andrew to pray for me. If one were so inclined, they could include the biblical Patriarchs, other Old and New Testament worthies, and other heroes from Christian history. I vary this group day to day, asking for intercession from whomever comes to mind in that moment.

I always close my Saint and Ancestral Intercession time with the Mother of Jesus. I ask her to seek mercies on my behalf from the Son whom she bore, that He may grant me my petitions.

I then return to prayer directed to our God. I tell Him once again that I surrender that day to His Will. I reiterate my petition that He grant me protection, blessings, strength, and guidance for my job and my other projects. And I pray the Trisagion one more time. And I close my prayer with the Sign of the Cross, "In the Name of the Father, and of the Son, and of the Holy Spirit."

Intercessory Prayer in Perspective

Keep in mind that, even though we may ask many other people to pray for us, living and deceased, we can never obtain anything through prayer that is not within God's Will for us. God tells Jeremiah the following:

> If Moses and Samuel were standing before me (praying), my spirit would not be toward this people. (Jer 15:1)

This means that we may bring numbers into our favor through intercessory prayer, but God's Will is always supreme. The fact that God wants us to pray for things and also the fact that God will never grant us anything outside His Will for us is quite liberating! It means we can and should freely pray for all the righteous desires of our heart, knowing and trusting that prayer is the means through which we can discern God's Will for what is best for us.

What If Our Ancestors Aren't In Heaven?

Here I've been telling you about asking our beloved dead to pray for us. But this is indeed a reasonable question What if our parents and ancestors aren't in heaven?

Before we return to that question, why do we feel the need to talk with them? Simple. We love them and miss them. My parents have been dead for a few years now. I still have not deleted their numbers off my cell phone. Nor will I. And that's because I used to call them when I wanted to tell them some news of my life or just to chat.

I still call them regularly in prayer. I talk to them and I believe they hear me. They visit me in my dreams from time to time. I pray for them and I ask them to pray for me.

So, back to the question. Where are my parents? On one level, intellectually, no one knows where the dead have gone. On another level, more importantly, in my heart I know that my parents are in heaven. And you know in your heart that your beloved dead are in the Bosom of Abraham. It's going to turn out that God's generosity in mercy and grace are beyond our comprehension. Oh, there is a Hell and there are souls in it. But it's a place where those who reject God's love and His grace persistently, even after their death, have actually elected to exist apart from His loving presence. That does not include our beloved dead.

So confidently talk to your ancestors. Share your joys, your triumphs, as well as your grief and your pains. Ask them to seek mercies on your behalf. Pray mercies upon them.

To Whom Should We Pray?

As I close this chapter on prayer, I want to address the matter of whom we should be addressing in prayer if we are Christians who profess a belief in the Trinity. We believe in One God, in Three Persons, Father, Son, and Holy Spirit. What does the Bible and early Christian practice teach us regarding how we should address prayer to our Creator?

Prayer Addressed to the Father

God is addressed as Father in the Old Testament:

> And now, O LORD, You are **our Father**; we are the clay and You are our potter and we are all the work of Your hand. (Isaiah 64:8)

In the New Testament, Jesus teaches us to address God generally as Father on numerous occasions, most notably in the Lord's Prayer:

Your Father knows what you need before you ask Him. Pray then in this way:
Our Father who art in Heaven... (Matthew 6:8-9)

St. Paul also teaches:

You have received the spirit of sonship. When we cry "**Abba! Father!**" the Spirit Himself bears witness with our spirit that we are children of God. (Romans 8:15-16)

Prayer to the Father in the Name of Jesus

So we certainly have been taught by both word and example to address God as Father in prayer. But Jesus additionally instructs us to ask the Father for things in prayer in His (Jesus') name:

Truly, truly I say to you, **if you ask the Father anything in my name He will give it to you**. Until now you have not asked anything in my name. Ask and you will receive, that your joy may be full. (John 16:23-24)

Prayer Addressed to Jesus

So certainly the Bible endorses prayer addressed to the Father. But what about praying directly to Jesus? While the nature of the Trinity, One God in Three Persons, is beyond human understanding, addressing a prayer to any member of that Trinity would seem valid. And the Bible does present us with examples of prayer directed to Jesus.

> Anything you ask in my name I will do. (John 14:14)

Some ancient manuscripts add the word "me" after "ask" here. That is understandable, because Jesus tells us that *He* will carry out anything we ask in His name.

St. Paul closes his 1st Letter to the Corinthians with a short Aramaic prayer:

> **Our Lord, come!** (maranatha) (1 Cor 16:22)

The Book of Revelation closes with a similar

short prayer:

> He who testifies to these things says,
> "Surely I am coming soon. Amen! **Come,
> Lord Jesus**! (Rev 22:20)

The Greek of the prayer found in Revelation 22:20 uses the vocative case of the word for "Lord," Kyrie. So it is certain here that Jesus is being directly addressed in the prayer.

St. Paul also describes Himself as praying directly to Jesus and receiving from Jesus a response:

> Three times **I asked the Lord** about this (the thorn in his flesh) that it would leave me; but He said to me, "My grace is enough for you, for **my power** is perfected in weakness." I will all the more gladly boast in my weaknesses, that **the power of Christ** may rest upon me.
> (2 Cor 12:8-9)

Prayer Addressed to the Holy Spirit?

Based on the principle that the Holy Spirit is fully God along with the Father and the Son, there would certainly be no offense intended or taken by God from addressing the Holy Spirit directly in prayer. But in the interest of full disclosure, I will point out that there is no early example of it in the Christian tradition.

There is no example of a prayer addressed directly to the Holy Spirit in the Bible. But the Bible does describe the Holy Spirit as having a crucial role in the power of our prayers. As I referred to above, St. Paul tells us:

> Likewise also the Spirit helps our weaknesses; for **we do not know how to pray as we ought,** but **the Spirit Himself intercedes for us with sighs that cannot be spoken.**
> (Romans 8:26)

St. Paul also tells us:

> Pray at all times **in the Spirit**, with all prayer and supplication. (Eph 6:18)

Examples of prayers addressed directly to the Holy Spirit did eventually appear in the Historical Church. In the Eastern Church, for instance, there is a prayer from the hymns of Pentecost:

> O Heavenly King, the Comforter, the Spirit of Truth, Who are everywhere and fills all things; Treasury of Blessings, and Giver of Life - come and abide in us, and cleanse us from every impurity, and save our souls, O Good One.

This is undoubtedly an example of a prayer addressed to the Holy Spirit. And the fact that it is an official part of the Church's Liturgies certainly endorses for Orthodox Christians the practice of praying directly to the Holy Spirit.

In the Western Church, prayers addressed directly to the Holy Spirit also found their way into use through hymns such as one written by St. Ambrose (AD 340-397):

> Come, Holy Spirit, Who ever One
> Are with the Father and the Son;

Come, Holy Spirit, our souls possess
With Thy full flood of holiness.

Conclusion: To Whom Should We Pray?

If we were to take all the verses of the Bible that I have quoted on this topic and also study the historical development of various liturgical norms and try then to produce one official way to address God in prayer, we would be completely missing the point of what our Loving God wants. He certainly does not want us to have any apprehension in our hearts about "whether we're doing it right."

We can rest in the grace that St. Paul already told us that "we do not know how to pray as we ought" (Romans 8:26). The Holy Spirit prays within us and washes away our inadequacy.

Perhaps the easiest thing for Christians to do is to address prayer generally to God, but close the prayer "in the name of the Father, and of the Son, and of the Holy Spirit" (Matt 28:19). If you ever feel in a particular moment moved to pray directly to the Father, or to Jesus, or the Holy Spirit, do so!

Again, I have said this before, prayer is not a Magic Formula. It's a chance to spend time with our Loving God and Father. So, be not afraid. Pray. Love.

We should never be in fear that the formulas of words we use somehow could make or break the hearing and acceptance of our prayers by our Loving God. Just talk to God. Pour out your heart and soul to Him. Talk to your beloved dead. You love them, and they love you. Ask them to seek mercies on your behalf. Ask mercy for them.

> God is Love, and he who abides in Love abides in God and God in him. (1 John 4:16) There is no fear in love, but perfect love casts out fear. (1 John 4:18)

CONCLUSION

We have explored the world of prayer as found in the Bible and early Jewish and Christian writers. We are children of a Loving God who calls each of us to communicate with Him as to a Father. He wants to give us all things that are for our good. And there are things within His Will for us that we can claim only through boldness and persistence in prayer.

But by the very nature of the People of God, we are not called individually to share communion only with God. Rather, we abide within a Communion of Saints. We help one another to grow in faith and love of God, offering and asking for prayers from one another. And these bonds of love are not severed by death. We can ask those who have gone before us to seek mercies on our behalf, just as we continue to pray for them out of love.

And foremost among these witness who surround us are the first Patriarchs of the Faith, worthies such as Abraham and his wife Sarah, Isaac and Rebeccah, Jacob, along with Leah and Rachel. Out of love for their children, both spiritual and physical, they will seek mercies before the face of God.

Our own precious ancestors who have gone before us to their rest also still love us and will readily seek mercies for us.

Others who have lived righteous lives and shown courage for the Faith can also be counted on to seek mercies for us when asked. First and Foremost among them, is the one who gave birth to God Himself. The Blessed Virgin Mary seeks mercies for us from the Son whom she bore. And Jesus honors His mother, according to the Commandments.

May God bless you and have mercy on you and all those whom you love, living and deceased. Amen

APPENDIX:
SHOULD YOU ASK THE DEAD
TO PRAY FOR YOU?

I will now describe *from Scripture* how the practice of asking the faithful departed to pray for us was a common and valid ancient practice and continues to be a source of spiritual blessing for us today.

I myself grew up in a Christian community that did not approve of asking the departed to pray for us. In the course of my scriptural and historical studies, I discovered that the practice had been largely misunderstood by us Protestants and was supported by both the Bible and early Jewish and Christian writers. I will present for you the arguments for and against the practice and let you make up your own mind.

If you are part of the Protestant tradition (as I

also once was), your religious leaders will tell you that the practices I describe in this book are wrong. They may even tell you they are demonic. I will treat in this chapter all the various verses of Holy Scripture they are likely to quote as they attempt to refute my claims. And I will tell you why they are simply wrong.

But I do want, out of Christian charity, to tell you that your leaders assert what they do out of a concern for your spiritual wellbeing. They sincerely care for you and want you to avoid practices they believe are wrong. They are, however and unfortunately, defending a position that has cut itself off from the life-blood of ancient and historical Christian practice as it was passed down from Jesus to the Apostles. I will explain all of these things in this chapter.

Prayers for the Dead

I've focused on addressing the deceased and asking them to pray for us. But I have also mentioned the practice of praying *for them* in this book. The Western Church has tended to view praying for the dead as something primarily associated with helping our loved ones through a state of purification called Purgatory. The Eastern Church also prays for the dead but is inclined to describe prayer for the dead as simply an act of love for them. I will not address the wider topic of Purgatory here, but I do want to show readers not acquainted with the concept that praying for the dead is fully biblical.

In 2nd Timothy 1:16-18, St. Paul makes mention of Onesiphorus, who seems from context to have died. Here is what he writes:

> May the Lord grant mercy to the household of Onesiphorus, for he often refreshed me. He was not ashamed of my chains, but when he arrived in Rome he looked for me eagerly and he found me. **May the Lord grant him mercy from the Lord on that day**.

St. Paul here makes a simple prayer that God grant mercy to the soul of a loved one who has fallen asleep. And I make that same simple prayer for all my ancestors, following his example.

I have not quoted in this book any of the books

that the Christian Church traditionally included in her Canon but which were removed by Protestant Churches at the time of the Reformation. If you are interested in seeing yet another defense of praying for the dead, see 2nd Maccabees 12:40-45.

The Argument Against Saint Intercession

The condemnation of Saint (and Ancestral) Intercession has historically involved the following claims.

> 1) Saint Intercession is wrong because we should only pray to God
> 2) We cannot know whether the dead hear our prayers
> 3) The practice is not described in the Bible
> 4) The practice is actually directly condemned in the Bible
> 5) We should not ask the departed to pray for us because we should have no mediator except Christ

I will demonstrate, from the Bible as my primary source, that none of these five claims are true. After addressing each of these claims directly,

I will then explain why, in the end, we may safely accept the practice of Saint Intercession *simply because* the Historical Church practiced it. In the end, after all the biblical arguments, I will show that rejecting the practice of the Historical Church is a rejection of the Bible itself. And so, let's look now at the claims against Saint Intercession.

1) Saint Intercession is wrong because we should only pray to God

When early Jews and Christians asked their ancestors to "seek mercies" on their behalf, they were not "praying" to them in the modern sense of that word.

Protestants in particular bristle at hearing people use the term "pray to saints" because the verb "to pray" has evolved in English to mean "speak to God." And so on their ears the phrase "pray to saints" sounds like Catholic and Orthodox have made the saints into minor deities, which is not at all the case.

In older English, "to pray" merely meant "to ask." Shakespeare repeatedly used the phrase "I pray thee" in dialogue between two humans, with the meaning simply of "I ask you."[32]

Even so, clearly the verb "to pray" has now taken on a divine connotation, and that is why in this book I carefully describe asking the deceased to pray for us using exactly those words "asking the deceased to pray for us."

And so, for the record, Saint Intercession is not prayer to a deity. There is One God. If someone's understanding of English insists that the verb "to pray" means only "to talk to God," then we do not "pray" to Saints! When we ask the departed to pray for us, we are doing the same thing as when we ask a living person to pray for us. A valid criticism would indeed involve whether that dead human can even hear the request for prayer. But it is not fair to condemn Saint Intercession on the grounds that it is turning the dead into gods.

---

[32] A Midsummer Night's Dream Act 3, Scene 1; Romeo and Juliet Act 3, Scene 1; Henry V Act 4, Scene 3.

2) We cannot know whether the dead hear our prayers

Before I do present biblical passages that tell us that the departed can indeed hear us when we ask them to pray for us, I would ask how do we know whether God even hears our prayers? We don't. But we must have faith. My point is, it is a natural and comfortable impulse to speak to our beloved dead who have gone to sleep in the Lord. Is it really so easy to believe in God and to believe He hears our prayers, but then difficult to believe in a God who grants us, out of Love, a continual communion with those we love but have gone to their reward?

The faithful departed are not gods. They are not omnipotent or omniscient by their own nature, so the only way they can hear us ask them to pray for us is if God grants them this blessing.

Fortunately, the Bible teaches us quite clearly that God has indeed granted them this precious gift, which deepens the Communion of the Saints, both living and dead.

Those who condemn Saint Intercession claim

that the Bible does not provide **any evidence whatsoever** that those in heaven can hear our prayers or know what is happening on the earth. Let's see if this claim is true.

Scripture Teaches That The Angels in Heaven Can Hear Us!

Consider the following.

> Jesus said, "There is joy before the angels of God over one sinner who repents." (Luke 15:10)

And so, the angels are indeed aware of what goes on in the human realm.

Here's another verse that proves the angels are well aware of what happens on Earth:

> See that you do not despise one of these little ones, for I tell you that in heaven their angels always behold the face of my Father who is in Heaven. (Matt 18:19).

Now, Jesus told us that those who have died will be "like angels in heaven." (Matt 22:30) And so, if the faithful departed are like angels, and the angels clearly do know what happens on earth, then it follows logically that the faithful departed know what happens here as well.

While this logical argument is valid, it would still be nice to find verses in the Bible directly describing the faithful departed as being aware of the prayers of those still on earth.

Scripture Teaches That
The Saints in Heaven Can Hear Us!

In the Book of Revelation, we read:

> Each of the elders held a harp and gold bowls filled with incense, which are the prayers of the holy ones. (Rev 5:8)

The "holy ones" here is evidently referring to the prayers of the "saints" of the Church, at this period still a reference to all Christians, living or deceased. [33] So the prayers of the "holy ones,"

---

33 For instance, we read in 2 Corinthians 1:1, "Paul, an Apostle of Christ Jesus by the will of God, and Timothy our

visible to those in heaven, are the prayers of the living.

We also read in the Book of Revelation:

> Another angel came and stood at the altar, holding a gold censer. He was given a large amount of incense to offer, **along with the prayers of all the holy ones**, on the gold altar which was before the throne. The smoke of the incense **along with the prayers of the holy ones went up before God from the hand of the angel**. (Rev 8:3-4)

The Book of Revelation further describes the early Christian martyrs as asking God when they would receive justice. They ask Him:

> How long will it be, holy and true master, before you sit in judgment and avenge our blood upon the inhabitants of the earth? (Rev 6:10)

---

brother, to the church of God that is in Corinth, **with all the saints** throughout Achaia.

This passage implies that the early Christian martyrs, in the presence of God, are well aware that they have not yet received the justice they feel they are due. How do they know this unless the faithful departed are, by the grace of God, allowed to know what happens on earth?

Yet More Evidence

The Rich Man asked Abraham to send Lazarus to warn his still living five brothers. Abraham replied:

They have Moses and the Prophets. Let them listen to them. (Luke 16:29)

Abraham in this parable is apparently well versed in the lives and activities of Moses and the Prophets, men who lived and served God hundreds of years after Abraham's own life and death.

The Most Important Evidence of All That The Faithful Departed Can Hear Us

Finally, and perhaps most importantly, St. Paul proves quite definitively that the faithful departed know what happens in the earthly realm when he teaches us:

> Now I know in part. Then I shall know just as I also am known. (1 Cor. 13:12)

When St. Paul writes, "just as I am known," he of course means just as God knows him. And if he is claiming that in the afterlife he will know "just as he is known," he is indeed claiming that the faithful departed will enjoy **secondary omniscience** of the world they have left.

What I mean by **secondary omniscience**, is that the faithful departed know all, not by their own power, but by the power of God.

And so, Holy Scripture describes the Faithful Departed (as well as the angels) as being aware of the world they have left. We may confidently say that, if we ask one of them to pray for us, they know of our request. Again, the Faithful Departed are not gods. They know nothing of their own power. By the grace of God they are made aware of communications to them.

And so, the claim that the Bible contains no evidence whatsoever that the faithful departed know what happens on earth is quite clearly wrong.

And so, let's examine the next claim against Saint Intercession.

3) The practice is not described in the Bible

Again, those who condemn Saint Intercession live in a world of absolutes. They are claiming the position that the Bible **contains no reference whatsoever to addressing the angels or the faithful departed**. And so, if we can find **even one example of it in the Bible, this claim is disproven**.

We read in Psalm 103:20:

> Bless the LORD, O you His angels, you mighty ones who do His word.

One could argue that an address to the angels in the book of Psalms is purely poetic, with no theological implication to be implied. Indeed, we also read in Psalm 148:2-3 another invocation of angels but also of inanimate objects:

> Praise Him, all His angels, praise Him, all His host! Praise Him, sun and moon, praise Him, all you shining stars!

Once again we face the issue that those who condemn Saint Intercession start by claiming there is no reference whatsoever on a certain topic. And then, when an example is shown, then some might decide there must be some reason to ignore it and declare that this particular example doesn't count.

The Faithful Departed Are Addressed in the New Testament!

What if the Bible itself gave us an example of addressing, not just the angels, but the blessed departed of our faith?

Read the following from the Book of Revelation 18:20, which describes the scene after the destruction of Babylon:

> Be glad over her, **O heaven, O saints, apostles, and prophets**, for God has given judgment for you against her.

This a clear example in the Bible advocating a direct address, not of angels poetically, but of the faithful dead of the Church. The parallel between "O heaven" and "O saints, apostles, and prophets" makes it unmistakable that this passage is depicting a direct address to the departed heroes of our faith.

So, far from providing **absolutely no evidence** whatsoever that those in heaven should be directly addressed, the Bible **abounds in it**.

On to the fourth claim condemning Saint Intercession.

4) The practice is actually directly condemned in the Bible

This claim is true if, and only if, Saint Intercession, as it is practiced in the Catholic and Orthodox Churches, is accurately described and then specifically condemned. In fact, the verses quoted by those who make this assertion are clear that they are not referring to Saint Intercession but something altogether different.

The Bible does indeed condemn the practice of necromancy, that is to say, consulting dead spirits in order to gain supernatural knowledge. This condemnation is found in Isaiah 8:19-20:

> When they say to you, "Consult (דרשו; **dirshu**) the mediums and the wizards who chirp and mutter." Should not a people consult (ידרש; **yidrosh**) their God instead of the dead on behalf of the living?

The Hebrew original of this passage makes it clear that what is condemned is specifically the practice of "consulting" the dead, that is to say, seeking (**darash**) knowledge and information from them.

The Hebrew Bible elsewhere condemns any contact with other practitioners of black magic who presumably engage in the same forbidden practices (Ex 22:18; Lev 19:26; Deut 18:10-11).

But addressing someone who is dead, asking them to pray for us, is simply not the same thing as practicing necromancy, seeking information from the realm of the dead.

If merely *speaking to the dead* is the same thing as the necromancy condemned in the Bible, then Jesus Himself would be guilty of the sin of necromancy (and liable to execution by stoning, Lev 20:27).

At the Transfiguration, Jesus spoke with Elijah and Moses (Matt 17:3). Elijah had been assumed into heaven and was arguably not dead. But Moses died (Deut 34:5). And then Jesus spoke with him. If merely speaking to the dead, under any circumstances, is necromancy, then Jesus would a necromancer.

Look, he's obviously not. And that's the point. The assertion that asking the faithful departed to pray for us is the necromancy condemned by the Bible is simply not true.

So, let's examine the final argument traditionally put forth as to why we should not ask the faithful departed to pray for us.

5) We should not ask the departed to pray for us because we should have no mediator except Christ

This claim stems from the same misunderstanding of the term "praying to Saints" we explored earlier. Let me state again. Saint Intercession is one human asking another human to pray for them. Granted, it is a living human asking a dead human to pray. But we discovered that the Bible itself explains why death should not prevent us from asking a loved one or a Saint from praying for us.

It is true that the Bible describes Jesus as the *only Mediator* between Man and God:

> **For there is one God, and there is one mediator between God and men**, the

man **Christ Jesus**, who gave Himself as a ransom for all. (1 Timothy 2:5-6)

If one human asking another human to pray is a rejection of Jesus' role as our sole Mediator, let's call out those who are guilty of this error.

St. Paul himself, in 1 Timothy 2:1.

That's right, just four verses before he declared that there is only one mediator between God and men, Jesus Christ, St. Paul, a human, asked other humans to pray:

> First of all, then, I ask that supplications, prayers, petitions, and thanksgivings be offered for everyone. (1 Timothy 2:1)

The fact that St. Paul himself, a human, asked other humans to pray just four verses before the statement that Jesus is the only Mediator between God and Man should convince all readers that asking another human to pray has nothing at all to do with Jesus as Mediator.

Here are yet other verses in which he asked people to pray, thereby, some would say, rejecting the concept of Jesus as Sole Mediator which he himself asserted in 1 Tim 2:5-6:

> Brethren, pray for us. (1 Thess 5:25)

> Be steadfast in prayer, being watchful in it with thanksgiving; and pray for us also. (Col 4:2-3)

Again, my point is that St. Paul himself abundantly asks people to pray for other people. One human asking another human to pray for them is not a rejection of the concept that Jesus is the Sole Mediator between God and Man. A human asking a deceased human for prayer is no more a violation of this than the next candidate guilty as charged.

Moses. When the people of Israel sinned, and God sent snakes among them, they came to Moses and declared:

> We sinned when we spoke against the LORD and against you. **Pray that the LORD will take away the snakes**. (Numbers 21:7)

And Moses prayed for them. And then God declared:

> Make a snake and put it on a pole. If anyone who has been bitten looks at it, he will live. (Numbers 21:8)

Notice that Moses does not reply to their request for prayer that he should **not** be a mediator between them and God. And notice that God hears Moses' prayer and grants the people grace within their punishment. God does **not** tell Moses that he will not hear his prayer because the people should have only prayed directly to him.

In other words, God does not at all reject the idea that one human should be the **prayer intermediary** for other humans. Whether the deceased can hear us is a separate matter I discussed earlier. But that the fact that someone is deceased does not somehow make asking them to pray for us a denial of Jesus' unique mediation.

Safety in the Pillar and Base of the Truth

We've just explored the common criticisms of Saint Intercession asserted by those who reject the practice. And I started this chapter by running through those verses because I know that readers from communities that don't practice Saint Intercession do need to see an alternative view of the passages quoted to claim that Saint Intercession is unbiblical.

But now I want to explain why all of that was ultimately unnecessary. The Church in the earliest centuries of Christian history supported and practiced Saint Intercession. I've shown that the Bible does not condemn this practice and contains verses that establish the possibility that those in heaven can hear us and would pray for us if asked. But there is an even more trustworthy way to confidently accept this practice.

It is a matter of historical record that the entire Christian Church in, say, the year AD 800 practiced Saint Intercession. If someone teaches that the Church ***should not*** practice Saint Intercession, they presumably believe that the earliest Christian Church did not practice it and that Saint Intercession crept into the Church's practice as an error somewhere between the Day of Pentecost and AD 800. **But the implication of that belief is that the entire Christian Church *could* fall into error.** Let's explore whether the Bible would allow us to hold that belief.

What does the Bible have to say about the Church?

The word "Church" (*εκκλησια: ekklesia*) occurs numerous times in the Epistles, but only twice in the Gospels. Yet these two references from the Gospels tell us much about the nature of the Church which Jesus founded.

Peter proclaims that Jesus is the Christ, the Son of the Living God. Jesus responds:

> You are Peter (***Petros***), and on this Rock (***petra***) I will build my Church. **And the Gates of Hell shall not prevail against it**. (Matt 16:18)

Jesus says here that the Gates of Hell **shall not prevail against the Church**. He does not say here that the Church will remain in the truth by following the Bible.

If the Church did fall into horrible errors for *centuries*, how could we believe that the Gates of Hell did not prevail against it?

Where was Jesus during the centuries in which the Church supposedly taught the errors that Protestants believe were corrected only starting in the 1500's? Why did the Germans in the 1500's deserve to get the True Church restored and not the Italians in the 700's?

Here's the other use of the word "Church" in the Gospels. In Matthew 18:15-17, Jesus describes a scenario in which a Christian brother or sister is in sin. He says that first you are to tell them about their fault alone. And if they listen (and repent), then you have gained back your brother or sister. If they do not listen, you are to go back with two or three witnesses. And if they still do not listen:

Tell it to the Church; and if he refuses to listen **even to the Church**, let him be to you as a Gentile and a tax collector. (Matthew 18:17)

Notice here that Jesus describes "The Church" as something capable of having an authoritative opinion. According to Jesus, the process of confronting a sinful member of the community is not going to them and quoting the Bible. **The Church, in Jesus' description, has the ability to speak *authoritatively*.** There is no way "The Church" could have this unless "The Church" has leaders authorized to decide and act for it.

And so, "The Church" that Jesus describes in the Gospels has the promise of victory over the Gates of Hell and the ability to speak with authority in the face of sin.

That's a far cry from the error-ridden Church some believe existed for over a thousand years.

Through the Church...

I have stated in this book that I was raised in the Lutheran Church. After college, I attended a Lutheran seminary with the intention of becoming a Lutheran minister. But I discovered, in the course of my studies, two verses of the Bible that shook me to the core. They have to do with the Church and whether it is the Church or the Bible that has the authority to teach us how to practice the Christian faith.

I had committed myself while at seminary to the discipline of reading the entire Bible, a thing I had never done, even though I was a seminary student. I had finished reading the Old Testament, I had finished the Gospels, and had entered the Epistles of St. Paul. That's when I stumbled on the following verse:

> That the manifold wisdom of God may now be made known **through the Church**."
> (Ephesians 3:10)

I can remember shaking my head, assuming, believing, even hoping that the original Greek of this passage somehow meant something other than what the English translation had said. I mean, if the Church is really **the means through which** the manifold wisdom of God is made known, well, that would mean the Church would have to be preserved in truth. That would mean that the belief of my Lutheran Church that the historical Church fell into many errors would be impossible.

I grabbed my Greek New Testament and took a look:

Through the Church
δια της εκκλησιας (**dia tes ekklesias**)

It was exactly what I feared. The Greek preposition δια (**dia**) simply means 'through', 'by means of'. For instance, we read in John 17:20:

> I do not ask on behalf of these alone, but for those also who will believe in Me **through** their word (δια του λογου αυτων; **dia tou logou auton**)

Through. By means of.

I expected the Bible to teach me that the manifold wisdom of God would be made know **through the Bible**! But instead the Bible itself teaches that it is made known through the Church!

I set this problem aside and went on with my life. And I continued my reading. And after just a few days, I stumbled on yet another land mine.

In my reading, I had reached 1st Timothy. And St. Paul wrote to St. Timothy the purpose of his letter was so that, in case he was delayed in making a personal visit:

> ...so that you will know how one ought to conduct himself in **the household of God**, which is **the church of the living God**, **the pillar and base of the truth**. (1 Tim 3:15)

I read these words and I was initially confused. What's the pillar and bulwark of the truth here? It must be God, right? I mean, that would make sense. "The church of the living God, (who is) the Pillar and Base of the Truth."

And then I suddenly realized that the original

Greek of this passage would be clear as to who or what was that Pillar and Base. I knew from the English that the Greek for "Church" must be in the Nominative Case, since it was the subject of the verb "is." And I knew that the phrase "of the living God" would be in what is called the Genitive Case. (Languages like Greek and Latin have special endings used to express the subjects of verbs and possession called the Genitive Case.)

And I knew that if God was the "Pillar and Base of the Truth," the words for that in Greek would have to also be in the Genitive Case. But if they were in the Nominative Case, then they were describing an attribute of the Church.

I can still remember the scene. My hands were shaking as I reached for my Greek New Testament. I needed those words to be in the Genitive.

But they weren't.

> **the church of the living God, the pillar and base of the truth.** (1 Tim 3:15) εκκλησια θεου ζωντος **στυλος και εδραιωμα** της αληθειας (ekklesia theou zontos **stylos kai edraioma** tes alethias)

Those words were in the Nominative Case, and so they were describing an attribute of the Church. St. Paul described ***the Church*** as the "Pillar and Base of the Truth."

Does the Bible describe the Church anywhere else as being incapable of falling into error?

The Bible clearly teaches that the Church is the New Covenant described in the Book of Jeremiah. The Epistle to the Hebrews makes this clear when it quotes from Jeremiah as fulfilled in the Church:

> I will make a New Covenant with the House of Israel (Hebrews 8:8, quoting Jeremiah 31:31)

And Hebrews explains that, in this New Covenant, the Church will be an institution in which the Truth will be instilled within the hearts of the believers:

> I will put my laws into their minds, and write them on their hearts (Hebrews 8:10, quoting Jeremiah 31:33)

Jeremiah further describes the nature of this New Covenant community as being unable to turn away from God and falling into error:

> I will give them **one heart and one way**. I will make with them an Everlasting Covenant, that I will not turn away from doing good to them; and I will put the fear of me in their hearts, **so that they will not turn away from me**. (Jeremiah 32:39-40)

How can any Christian read these verses and then imagine that the Church could fall systematically into error for centuries?

And so, if the Church did not fall into error, what are the implications of this? Simple. The practices that may not have been openly stated in Scripture, but which emerged as universal Christian practice, things like prayers for the dead and asking the faithful departed to pray for us, are a part of the Christian tradition and are validated as proper to our Faith.

So, have no worries as you follow the love in your heart and speak to your beloved dead. The Bible does not forbid it. Indeed, the Bible supports it. The Church does not forbid it. Indeed, the Church from the earliest centuries practiced it and endorsed it. And the teaching of the Church is the pillar and base upon which you can confidently rest your faith.